Professional Resumes Series

RESUMES
FOR
EDUCATION
CAREERS

The Editors of
VGM Career Horizons

Printed on recyclable paper

VGM Career Horizons
a division of *NTC Publishing Group*
Lincolnwood, Illinois USA

Library of Congress Cataloging-in-Publication Data

Résumés for education careers.

     p.   cm. — (VGM's professional résumés series)
  ISBN 0-8442-8543-9
    1. Résumés (Employment) 2. Teaching—Vocational guidance.
I. VGM Career Horizons (Firm) II. Series.
HF5383.R436 1992
650.14'02437—dc20   92-196
                                                  CIP

1994 Printing

Published by VGM Career Horizons, a division of NTC Publishing Group.
© 1992 by NTC Publishing Group, 4255 West Touhy Avenue,
Lincolnwood (Chicago), Illinois 60646-1975 U.S.A.

   4 5 6 7 8 9 0 VP 9 8 7 6 5 4 3

ACKNOWLEDGMENT

The editors gratefully acknowledge Margaret Gisler and Jeffrey S. Johnson for their help in the writing and production of this book.

CONTENTS

Introduction

Your resume is your first impression on a prospective employer. Though you may be articulate, intelligent, and charming in person, a poor resume may prevent you from ever having the opportunity to demonstrate your interpersonal skills, because a poor resume may prevent you from ever being called for an interview. While few people have ever been hired solely on the basis of their resume, a well-written, well-organized resume can go a long way toward helping you land an interview. Your resume's main purpose is to get you that interview. The rest is up to you and the employer. If you both feel that you are right for the job and the job is right for you, chances are you will be hired.

A resume must catch the reader's attention yet still be easy to read and to the point. Resume styles have changed over the years. Today, brief and focused resumes are preferred. No longer do employers have the patience, or the time, to review several pages of solid type. A resume should be only one page long, if possible, and never more than two pages. Time is a precious commodity in today's business world and the resume that is concise and straightforward will usually be the one that gets noticed.

Let's not make the mistake, though, of assuming that writing a brief resume means that you can take less care in preparing it. A successful resume takes time and thought, and if you are willing to make the effort, the rewards are well worth it. Think of your resume as a sales tool with the product being you. You want to sell yourself to a prospective employer. This book is designed to help you prepare a resume that will help you further your career—to land that next job, or first job, or to return to the work force after years of absence. So, read on. Make the effort and reap the rewards that a strong resume can bring to your career. Let's get to it!

Chapter One

THE ELEMENTS OF A GOOD RESUME

A winning resume is made of the elements that employers are most interested in seeing when reviewing a job applicant. These basic elements are the essential ingredients of a successful resume and become the actual sections of your resume. The following is a list of elements that may be used in a resume. Some are essential; some are optional. We will be discussing these in this chapter in order to give you a better understanding of each element's role in the makeup of your resume:

1. Heading
2. Objective
3. Work Experience
4. Education
5. Honors
6. Activities
7. Certificates and Licenses
8. Professional Memberships
9. Special Skills
10. Personal Information
11. References

The first step in preparing your resume is to gather together information about yourself and your past accomplishments. Later you will refine this information, rewrite it in the most effective language, and organize it into the most attractive layout. First, let's take a look at each of these important elements individually.

Heading

The heading may seem to be a simple enough element in your resume, but be careful not to take it lightly. The heading should be placed at the top of your resume and should include your name, home address, and telephone numbers. If you can take calls at your current place of business, include your business number, since most employers will attempt to contact you during the business day. If this is not possible, or if you can afford it, purchase an answering machine that allows you to retrieve your messages while you are away from home. This way you can make sure you don't miss important phone calls. *Always* include your phone number on your resume. It is crucial that when prospective employers need to have immediate contact with you, they can.

Objective

When seeking a particular career path, it is important to list a job objective on your resume. This statement helps employers know the direction that you see yourself heading, so that they can determine whether your goals are in line with the position available. The objective is normally one sentence long and describes your employment goals clearly and concisely. See the sample resumes in this book for examples of objective statements.

The job objective will vary depending on the type of person you are, the field you are in, and the type of goals you have. It can be either specific or general, but it should always be to the point.

In some cases, this element is not necessary, but usually it is a good idea to include your objective. It gives your possible future employer an idea of where you are coming from and where you want to go.

The objective statement is better left out, however, if you are uncertain of the exact title of the job you seek. In such a case, the inclusion of an overly specific objective statement could result in your not being considered for a variety of acceptable positions; you should be sure to incorporate this information in your cover letter, instead.

Work Experience

This element is arguably the most important of them all. It will provide the central focus of your resume, so it is necessary that this section be as complete as possible. Only by examining your work experience in depth can you get to the heart of your accomplishments and present them in a way that demonstrates the strength of your qualifications. Of course, someone just out of school will have less work experience than someone who has been working for a number of years, but the amount of information isn't the most important thing—rather, how it is presented and how it highlights you as a person and as a worker will be what counts.

As you work on this section of your resume, be aware of the need for accuracy. You'll want to include all necessary information about each of your jobs, including job title, dates, employer, city, state, responsibilities, special projects, and accomplishments. Be sure to only list company accomplishments for which you were directly responsible. If you haven't participated in any special projects, that's all right—this area may not be relevant to certain jobs.

The most common way to list your work experience is in *reverse chronological order.* In other words, start with your most recent job and work your way backwards. This way your prospective employer sees your current (and often most important) job before seeing your past jobs. Your most recent position, if the most important, should also be the one that includes the most information, as compared to your previous positions. If you are just out of school, show your summer employment and part-time work, though in this case your education will most likely be more important than your work experience.

The following worksheets will help you gather information about your past jobs.

WORK EXPERIENCE
Job One:

Job Title _____

Dates _____

Employer _____

City, State _____

Major Duties _____

_____

_____

_____

_____

_____

_____

_____

Special Projects _____

_____

_____

_____

Accomplishments _____

_____

_____

_____

_____

_____

_____

_____

_____

Job Two:

Job Title _____

Dates _____

Employer _____

City, State _____

Major Duties _____

_____

_____

_____

_____

_____

_____

Special Projects _____

_____

_____

_____

Accomplishments _____

_____

_____

_____

_____

_____

_____

_____

Job Three:

Job Title _____

Dates _____

Employer _____

City, State _____

Major Duties _____

_____

_____

_____

_____

_____

_____

_____

Special Projects _____

_____

_____

_____

Accomplishments _____

_____

_____

_____

_____

_____

_____

_____

Job Four:

Job Title _____

Dates _____

Employer _____

City, State _____

Major Duties _____

_____

_____

_____

_____

_____

_____

_____

Special Projects _____

_____

_____

_____

Accomplishments _____

_____

_____

_____

_____

_____

_____

_____

Education

Education is the second most important element of a resume. Your educational background is often a deciding factor in an employer's decision to hire you. Be sure to stress your accomplishments in school with the same finesse that you stressed your accomplishments at work. If you are looking for your first job, your education will be your greatest asset, since your work experience will most likely be minimal. In this case, the education section becomes the most important. You will want to be sure to include any degrees or certificates you received, your major area of concentration, any honors, and any relevant activities. Again, be sure to list your most recent schooling first. If you have completed graduate-level work, begin with that and work in reverse chronological order through your undergraduate education. If you have completed an undergraduate degree, you may choose whether to list your high school experience or not. This should be done only if your high school grade-point average was well above average.

The following worksheets will help you gather information for this section of your resume. Also included are supplemental worksheets for honors and for activities. Sometimes honors and activities are listed in a section separate from education, most often near the end of the resume.

EDUCATION

School _____

Major or Area of Concentration _____

Degree _____

Date _____

School _____

Major or Area of Concentration _____

Degree _____

Date _____

Honors

Here, you should list any awards, honors, or memberships in honorary societies that you have received. Usually these are of an academic nature, but they can also be for special achievement in sports, clubs, or other school activities. Always be sure to include the name of the organization honoring you and the date(s) received. Use the worksheet below to help gather your honors information.

HONORS

Honor: _____

Awarding Organization: _____

Date(s): _____

Honor: _____

Awarding Organization: _____

Date(s): _____

Honor: _____

Awarding Organization: _____

Date(s): _____

Honor: _____

Awarding Organization: _____

Date(s): _____

Activities

You may have been active in different organizations or clubs during your years at school; often an employer will look at such involvement as evidence of initiative and dedication. Your ability to take an active role, and even a leadership role, in a group should be included on your resume. Use the worksheet provided to list your activities and accomplishments in this area. In general, you should exclude any organization the name of which indicates the race, creed, sex, age, marital status, color, or nation of origin of its members.

ACTIVITIES

Organization/Activity: _____

Accomplishments: _____

_____

_____

Organization/Activity: _____

Accomplishments: _____

_____

_____

Organization/Activity: _____

Accomplishments: _____

_____

_____

Organization/Activity: _____

Accomplishments: _____

_____

_____

As your work experience increases through the years, your school activities and honors will play less of a role in your resume, and eventually you will most likely only list your degree and any major honors you received. This is due to the fact that, as time goes by, your job performance becomes the most important element in your resume. Through time, your resume should change to reflect this.

Certificates and Licenses

The next potential element of your resume is certificates and licenses. You should list these if the job you are seeking requires them and you, of course, have acquired them. If you have applied for a license, but have not yet received it, use the phrase "application pending."

License requirements vary by state. If you have moved or you are planning to move to another state, be sure to check with the appropriate board or licensing agency in the state in which you are applying for work to be sure that you are aware of all licensing requirements.

Always be sure that all of the information you list is completely accurate. Locate copies of your licenses and certificates and check the exact date and name of the accrediting agency. Use the following worksheet to list your licenses and certificates.

CERTIFICATES AND LICENSES

Name of License: _____

Licensing Agency: _____

Date Issued: _____

Name of License: _____

Licensing Agency: _____

Date Issued: _____

Name of License: _____

Licensing Agency: _____

Date Issued: _____

Professional Memberships

Another potential element in your resume is a section listing professional memberships. Use this section to list involvement in professional associations, unions, and similar organizations. It is to your advantage to list any professional memberships that pertain to the job you are seeking. Be sure to include the dates of your involvement and whether you took part in any special activities or held any offices within the organization. Use the following worksheet to gather your information.

PROFESSIONAL MEMBERSHIPS

Name of Organization: _____

Offices Held: _____

Activities: _____

Date(s): _____

Name of Organization: _____

Offices Held: _____

Activities: _____

Date(s): _____

Name of Organization: _____

Offices Held: _____

Activities: _____

Date(s): _____

Name of Organization: _____

Offices Held: _____

Activities: _____

Date(s): _____

Special Skills

This section of your resume is set aside for mentioning any special abilities you have that could relate to the job you are seeking. This is the part of your resume where you have the opportunity to demonstrate certain talents and experiences that are not necessarily a part of your educational or work experience. Common examples include fluency in a foreign language, or <u>knowledge of a particular computer application.</u>

Special skills can encompass a wide range of your talents—remember to be sure that whatever skills you list relate to the type of work you are looking for.

Personal Information

Some people include "Personal" information on their resumes. This is not generally recommended, but you might wish to include it if you think that something in your personal life, such as a hobby or talent, has some bearing on the position you are seeking. This type of information is often referred to at the beginning of an interview, when it is used as an "ice breaker." Of course, personal information regarding age, marital status, race, religion, or sexual preference should never appear on any resume.

References

HOSTS- Include Pattie's name in cover letter.

<u>References are not usually listed on the resume,</u> but a prospective employer needs to know that you have references who may be contacted if necessary. All that is necessary to include in your resume regarding references is a sentence at the bottom stating, "<u>References are available upon request.</u>" If a prospective employer requests a list of references, be sure to have one ready. Also, check with whomever you list to see if it is all right for you to use them as a reference. Forewarn them that they may receive a call regarding a reference for you. This way they can be prepared to give you the best reference possible.

Chapter Two

WRITING YOUR RESUME

*N*ow that you have gathered together all of the information for each of the sections of your resume, it's time to write out each section in a way that will get the attention of whoever is reviewing it. The type of language you use in your resume will affect its success. You want to take the information you have gathered and translate it into a language that will cause a potential employer to sit up and take notice.

Resume writing is not like expository writing or creative writing. It embodies a functional, direct writing style and focuses on the use of action words. By using action words in your writing, you more effectively stress past accomplishments. Action words help demonstrate your initiative and highlight your talents. Always use verbs that show strength and reflect the qualities of a "doer." By using action words, you characterize yourself as a person who takes action, and this will impress potential employers.

The following is a list of verbs commonly used in resume writing. Use this list to choose the action words that can help your resume become a strong one:

administered	introduced
advised	invented
analyzed	maintained
arranged	managed
assembled	met with
assumed responsibility	motivated
billed	negotiated
built	operated
carried out	orchestrated
channeled	ordered
collected	organized
communicated	oversaw
compiled	performed
completed	planned
conducted	prepared
contacted	presented
contracted	produced
coordinated	programmed
counseled	published
created	purchased
cut	recommended
designed	recorded
determined	reduced
developed	referred
directed	represented
dispatched	researched
distributed	reviewed
documented	saved
edited	screened
established	served as
expanded	served on
functioned as	sold
gathered	suggested
handled	supervised
hired	taught
implemented	tested
improved	trained
inspected	typed
interviewed	wrote

Now take a look at the information you put down on the work experience worksheets. Take that information and rewrite it in paragraph form, using verbs to highlight your actions and accomplishments. Let's look at an example, remembering that what matters here is the writing style, and not the particular job responsibilities given in our sample.

WORK EXPERIENCE
Regional Sales Manager

Manager of sales representatives from seven states. Responsible for twelve food chain accounts in the East. In charge of directing the sales force in planned selling toward specific goals. Supervisor and trainer of new sales representatives. Consulting for customers in the areas of inventory management and quality control.

Special Projects: Coordinator and sponsor of annual food industry sales seminar.

Accomplishments: Monthly regional volume went up 25 percent during my tenure while, at the same time, a proper sales/cost ratio was maintained. Customer/company relations improved significantly.

all libraries automated - technology implemented in curriculum areas

Below is the rewritten version of this information, using action words. Notice how much stronger it sounds.

WORK EXPERIENCE
Regional Sales Manager

Managed sales representatives from seven states. Handled twelve food chain accounts in the eastern United States. Directed the sales force in planned selling towards specific goals. Supervised and trained new sales representatives. Consulted for customers in the areas of inventory management and quality control. Coordinated and sponsored the annual Food Industry Seminar. Increased monthly regional volume 25 percent and helped to improve customer/company relations during my tenure.

Another way of constructing the work experience section is by using actual job descriptions. Job descriptions are rarely written using the proper resume language, but they do include all the information necessary to create this section of your resume. Take the description of one of the jobs your are including on your resume (if you have access to it), and turn it into an action-oriented paragraph. Below is an example of a job description followed by a version of the same description written using action words. Again, pay attention to the style of writing, as the details of your own work experience will be unique.

PUBLIC ADMINISTRATOR I

Responsibilities: Coordinate and direct public services to meet the needs of the nation, state, or community. Analyze problems; work with special committees and public agencies; recommend solutions to governing bodies.

Aptitudes and Skills: Ability to relate to and communicate with people; solve complex problems through analysis; plan, organize, and implement policies and programs. Knowledge of political systems; financial management; personnel administration; program evaluation; organizational theory.

WORK EXPERIENCE
Public Administrator I

Wrote pamphlets and conducted discussion groups to inform citizens of legislative processes and consumer issues. Organized and supervised 25 interviewers. Trained interviewers in effective communication skills.

Now that you have learned how to word your resume, you are ready for the next step in your quest for a winning resume: assembly and layout.

Chapter Three

ASSEMBLY AND LAYOUT

*A*t this point, you've gathered all the necessary information for your resume, and you've rewritten it using the language necessary to impress potential employers. Your next step is to assemble these elements in a logical order and then to lay them out on the page neatly and attractively in order to achieve the desired effect: getting that interview.

Assembly

The order of the elements in a resume makes a difference in its overall effect. Obviously, you would not want to put your name and address in the middle of the resume or your special skills section at the top. You want to put the elements in an order that stresses your most important achievements, not the less pertinent information. For example, if you recently graduated from school and have no full-time work experience, you will want to list your education before you list any part-time jobs you may have held during school. On the other hand, if you have been gainfully employed for several years and currently hold an important position in your company, you will want to list your work experience ahead of your education, which has become less pertinent with time.

There are some elements that are always included in your resume and some that are optional. Following is a list of essential and optional elements:

Essential	*Optional*
Name	Job Objective
Address	Honors
Phone Number	Special Skills
Work Experience	Professional Memberships
Education	Activities
References Phrase	Certificates and Licenses
	Personal Information

Your choice of optional sections depends on your own background and employment needs. Always use information that will put you and your abilities in a favorable light. If your honors are impressive, then be sure to include them in your resume. If your activities in school demonstrate particular talents necessary for the job you are seeking, then allow space for a section on activities. Each resume is unique, just as each person is unique.

Types of Resumes

So far, our discussion about resumes has involved the most common type—the *reverse chronological* resume, in which your most recent job is listed first and so on. This is the type of resume usually preferred by human resources directors, and it is the one most frequently used. However, in some cases this style of presentation is not the most effective way to highlight your skills and accomplishments.

For someone reentering the work force after many years or someone looking to change career fields, the *functional resume* may work best. This type of resume focuses more on achievement and less on the sequence of your work history. In the functional resume, your experience is presented by what you have accomplished and the skills you have developed in your past work.

A functional resume can be assembled from the same information you collected for your chronological resume. The main difference lies in how you organize this information. Essentially, the work experience section becomes two sections, with your job duties and accomplishments comprising one section and your employer's name, city, state, your position, and the dates employed making up another section. The first section is placed near the top of the resume, just below the job objective section, and can be called *Accomplishments* or *Achievements*. The second section, containing the bare essentials of your employment history, should come after the accomplishments section and can be titled *Work Experience* or *Employment History*. The other sections of your resume remain the same. The work experience section is the only one affected in the functional resume. By placing the section that focuses on your achievements first, you thereby draw attention to these achievements. This puts less emphasis on who you worked for and more emphasis on what you did and what you are capable of doing.

For someone changing careers, emphasis on skills and achievements is essential. The identities of previous employers, which may be unrelated to one's new job field, need to be downplayed. The functional resume accomplishes this task. For someone reentering the work force after many years, a functional resume is the obvious choice. If you lack full-time work experience, you will need to draw attention away from this fact and instead focus on your skills and abilities gained possibly through volunteer activities or part-time work. Education may also play a more important role in this resume.

Which type of resume is right for you will depend on your own personal circumstances. It may be helpful to create a chronological *and* a functional resume and then compare the two to find out which is more suitable. The sample resumes found in this book include both chronological and functional resumes. Use these resumes as guides to help you decide on the content and appearance of your own resume.

Layout

Once you have decided which elements to include in your resume and you have arranged them in an order that makes sense and emphasizes your achievements and abilities, then it is time to work on the physical layout of your resume.

There is no single appropriate layout that applies to every resume, but there are a few basic rules to follow in putting your resume on paper:

1. Leave a comfortable margin on the sides, top, and bottom of the page (usually 1 to 1½ inches).

2. Use appropriate spacing between the sections (usually 2 to 3 line spaces are adequate).

3. Be consistent in the *type* of headings you use for the different sections of your resume. For example, if you capitalize the heading EMPLOYMENT HISTORY, don't use initial capitals and underlining for a heading of equal importance, such as Education.

4. Always try to fit your resume onto one page. If you are having trouble fitting all your information onto one page, perhaps you are trying to say too much. Try to edit out any repetitive or unnecessary information or possibly shorten descriptions of earlier jobs. Be ruthless. Maybe you've included too many optional sections.

CHRONOLOGICAL RESUME

JOHN J. ALLEN

Present Address
765 5th Street
Washington, D.C. 20016-8001
(202) 555 - 2213

Permanent Address
28 Octavia Trail
Carmel, IN 46032
(317) 555 - 6675

OBJECTIVE
Full-time teaching position in telecommunications research and development, particularly in optical fiber networks, satellite communications or antenna design.

EDUCATION
University of Washington
Currently pursuing Masters of Science in Electrical Engineering with a concentration in telecommunications and fiber optics.
Expected Graduation: June, 1992

Whitman College
Bachelors of Science with Highest Distinction in Electrical Engineering, May, 1989

EXPERIENCE
1989-1990
University of Washington Dept. of Electrical Engineering
TEACHING ASSISTANT: Controls Courses and Intro to Electronics Lab.

Summer 1990
Amoco Incorporated, Washington, D.C.,
SPECIAL TECHNICAL ASSISTANT: Installed hardware and software for computer control of test equipment; conducted stress tests on circuit boards; wrote software to capture and plot oscilloscope waveforms.

Summer 1989
Naylor Pipe Company, Chicago, IL.
SENIOR STAFF TECHNOLOGIST: Conducted research on optical fiber communication systems. Primary research was an experimental study of privacy and security issues in passive, fiber-to-the-home networks.

ADDITIONAL INFORMATION
CAD tool experience: SPICE, MAGIC, IRSIM, and SUPREM
Member Tau Beta Pi and Pi Tau Sigma

FUNCTIONAL RESUME

Denise R. Jacobson
9270 Harvard Drive, Apartment A
Indianapolis, Indiana 46000
(317) 555-7979

Career Objective

A challenging position in administration which will utilize my organizational, leadership, and interpersonal skills in a middle/secondary school environment.

Education

Member of the Experiential Program for Preparing School Principals (Cohort Group 9) at Butler University, Indianapolis, Indiana. Expected completion date December 1991.

Master's Degree in Secondary Education from Indiana University-Purdue University in Indianapolis, Indiana. Degree received May 1988.

Bachelor of Arts Degree from Hanover College in Hanover, Indiana. Graduate cum laude in May 1982.

High School Diploma from South Ripley High School in Versailles, Indiana. Graduated with honors in May 1978.

Professional Experience

Presently teaching secondary mathematics at Lawrence North High School in Indianapolis, Indiana.

Taught evening mathematics classes at Indiana Vocational Technical College in Indianapolis, Indiana.

Taught secondary mathematics and basic programming courses at Triton Central High School in Fairland, Indiana.

Extracurricular Responsibilities

Member of the Performance Based Accreditation Steering Committee at Lawrence North High School.

Committee member for the School Improvement Program #4 at Lawrence North High School.

Member of the Lawrence Education Association Discussion Team for the previous three years.

Mentor for a beginning teacher during the 1990-1991 school year at Lawrence North High School.

Student Council co-sponsor for the past four years.

Don't let the idea of having to tell every detail about your life get in the way of producing a resume that is simple and straightforward. The more compact your resume, the easier it will be to read and the better an impression it will make for you.

In some cases, the resume will not fit on a single page, even after extensive editing. In such cases, the resume should be printed on two pages so as not to compromise clarity or appearance. Each page of a two-page resume should be marked clearly with your name and the page number, e.g., "Judith Ramirez, page 1 of 2." The pages should then be stapled together.

Try experimenting with various layouts until you find one that looks good to you. Always show your final layout to other people and ask them what they like or dislike about it, and what impresses them most about your resume. Make sure that is what you want most to emphasize. If it isn't, you may want to consider making changes in your layout until the necessary information is emphasized. Use the sample resumes in this book to get some ideas for laying out your resume.

Putting Your Resume in Print

Your resume should be typed or printed on good quality $8^{1}/_{2}'' \times 11''$ bond paper. You want to make as good an impression as possible with your resume; therefore, quality paper is a necessity. If you have access to a word processor with a good printer, or know of someone who does, make use of it. Typewritten resumes should only be used when there are no other options available.

After you have produced a clean original, you will want to make duplicate copies of it. Usually a copy shop is your best bet for producing copies without smudges or streaks. Make sure you have the copy shop use quality bond paper for all copies of your resume. Ask for a sample copy before they run your entire order. After copies are made, check each copy for cleanliness and clarity.

Another more costly option is to have your resume typeset and printed by a printer. This will provide the most attractive resume of all. If you anticipate needing a lot of copies of your resume, the cost of having it typeset may be justified.

Proofreading

After you have finished typing the master copy of your resume and before you go to have it copied or printed, you must thoroughly check it for typing and spelling errors. Have several people read it over just in case you may have missed an error. Misspelled words and typing mistakes will not make a good impression on a prospective employer, as they are a bad reflection on your writing ability and your attention to detail. With thorough and conscientious proofreading, these mistakes can be avoided.

The following are some rules of capitalization and punctuation that may come in handy when proofreading your resume:

Rules of Capitalization

- Capitalize proper nouns, such as names of schools, colleges, and universities, names of companies, and brand names of products.

- Capitalize major words in the names and titles of books, tests, and articles that appear in the body of your resume.

- Capitalize words in major section headings of your resume.

- Do not capitalize words just because they seem important.

- When in doubt, consult a manual of style such as *Words Into Type* (Prentice-Hall), or *The Chicago Manual of Style* (The University of Chicago Press). Your local library can help you locate these and other reference books.

Rules of Punctuation

- Use a comma to separate words in a series.

- Use a semicolon to separate series of words that already include commas within the series.

- Use a semicolon to separate independent clauses that are not joined by a conjunction.

- Use a period to end a sentence.

- Use a colon to show that the examples or details that follow expand or amplify the preceding phrase.

- Avoid the use of dashes.

- Avoid the use of brackets.

- If you use any punctuation in an unusual way in your resume, be consistent in its use.

- Whenever you are uncertain, consult a style manual.

Chapter Four

THE COVER LETTER

*O*nce your resume has been assembled, laid out, and printed to your satisfaction, the next and final step before distribution is to write your cover letter. Though there may be instances where you deliver your resume in person, most often you will be sending it through the mail. Resumes sent through the mail always need an accompanying letter that briefly introduces you and your resume. The purpose of the cover letter is to get a potential employer to read your resume, just as the purpose of your resume is to get that same potential employer to call you for an interview.

Like your resume, your cover letter should be clean, neat, and direct. A cover letter usually includes the following information:

1. Your name and address.

2. The date.

3. The name and address of the person and company to whom you are sending your resume.

4. The salutation ("Dear Mr." or "Dear Ms." followed by the person's last name, or "To Whom It May Concern").

5. An opening paragraph explaining why you are writing (in response to an ad, the result of a previous meeting, at the suggestion of someone you both know) and indicating your interest in the job being offered.

6. One or two more paragraphs that tell why you want to work for the company and what qualifications and experience you can bring to that company.

7.   A final paragraph that closes the letter and requests that you be contacted for an interview. You may mention here that your references are available upon request.

8.   The closing ("Sincerely," or "Yours Truly," followed by your signature with your name typed under it).

Your cover letter, including all of the information above, should be no more than one page in length. The language used should be polite, businesslike, and to the point. Do not attempt to tell your life story in the cover letter. A long and cluttered letter will only serve to put off the reader. Remember, you only need to mention a few of your accomplishments and skills in the cover letter. The rest of your information is in your resume. Each and every achievement should not be mentioned twice. If your cover letter is a success, your resume will be read and all pertinent information reviewed by your prospective employer.

Producing the Cover Letter

Cover letters should always be typed individually, since they are always written to particular individuals and companies. Never use a form letter for your cover letter. Each one should be as personal as possible. Of course, once you have written and rewritten your first cover letter to the point where you are satisfied with it, you certainly can use similar wording in subsequent letters.

After you have typed your cover letter on quality bond paper, be sure to proofread it as thoroughly as you did your resume. Again, spelling errors are a sure sign of carelessness, and you don't want that to be a part of your first impression on a prospective employer. Make sure to handle the letter and resume carefully to avoid any smudges, and then mail both your cover letter and resume in an appropriate sized envelope. Be sure to keep an accurate record of all the resumes you send out and the results of each mailing.

Numerous sample cover letters appear at the end of the book. Use them as models for your own cover letter or to get an idea of how cover letters are put together. Remember, every one is unique and depends on the particular circumstances of the individual writing it and the job for which he or she is applying.

About a week after mailing resumes and cover letters to potential employers, you will want to contact them by telephone. Confirm that your resume arrived, and ask whether an interview might be possible. Getting your foot in the door during this call is half the battle of a job search, and a strong resume and cover letter will help you immeasurably.

Chapter Five

SAMPLE RESUMES

This chapter contains dozens of sample resumes for people pursuing a wide variety of jobs and careers in education. There are many different styles of resumes in terms of graphic layout and presentation of information. These samples also represent people with varying amounts of education and work experience. Use these samples to model your own resume after. Choose one resume, or borrow elements from several different resumes to help you construct your own.

PATRICIA YOUNG
66 Chambers Rd.
Hartford, CT 00112
203/555-2229

OBJECTIVE: High School Teacher

EDUCATION: <u>HARTFORD COLLEGE</u>, Hartford, CT
                             B.A. in Secondary Education, 1991
                             Minor: Spanish

COURSEWORK: Principles of Education
                             Principles of Secondary Education
                             American Literature
                             Spanish
                             Career Counseling
                             Secondary Administration
                             Special Education
                             Comparative Literature
                             Spanish Literature

STUDENT TEACHING: <u>CENTRAL HIGH SCHOOL</u>, Hartford, CT
                             Taught Spanish I, 1990, 1991
                             Supervised discussion section of Spanish Literature, 1991

ACTIVITIES: Secretary, Associated Student Government
                             President, Spanish Club
                             Tennis Team

References submitted upon request

PHILOSOPHY OF EDUCATION

Education, to me, is more than just textbook knowledge, it is also personal life skills gained in the classroom. While it is a teacher's job to cover the curriculum, it is also the teacher's responsibility to develop the whole child. By this I mean that a teacher should be concerned with a child's emotional, mental, physical, and cognitive abilities.

To me, school is more than just a building where reading, writing, and arithmetic are taught; it is a place of growth and learning. Here is where a child learns to socialize, respect others, develop high self-esteem, learn discipline, and responsibility. It is at school that every child is given the chance to develop and learn.

I believe that learning is possible for all children, as is success, but it is the result of time and patience. Teachers should have high expectations for all students; however, teachers need to be careful not to frustrate the lower achievers. If teachers encourage learning and make it worthwhile, I believe that learning will flourish in the classroom.

Children learn in different ways. Because all children deserve an equal chance to learn, it is the responsibility of the teacher to meet these different learning styles to the best of his/her ability. This is done by presenting the material in a variety of ways, as well as incorporating as many hands-on experiences as possible. I believe children will retain material better if they experience it. I also feel students should be shown the relevancy of subject material to life.

I believe that education is more than just teaching; it is loving, caring, showing, communicating, and growing. By implementing all these parts into the educational program, the teacher can help children dream and reach those dreams. I also believe that if all this is to occur, open lines of communication need to be present between parents, teachers, and principals. Everyone needs to be involved if the development of the whole child is to take place.

MARY OLIVE LIEN
1456 Howard Drive
Cincinnati, Ohio 45642
(513) 555 - 8972

CAREER OBJECTIVE_____

Seeking an elementary teaching position.
Seeking a junior high/middle school Spanish position.
Seeking a volleyball coaching position.

RELEVANT EXPERIENCE_____

Student Teaching

Phase 1   Pioneer Trails Elementary, Cincinnati, OH
          Fourth Grade, Open Concept.

Phase 2   Northview Middle School, Middletown, OH
          Seventh and Eighth Grade Spanish.

OTHER EXPERIENCE_____
                                                          United
Student Aid Funds, Cincinnati, OH
Business Intern in Fraud/Abuse Division
Investigated fraudulent loans with Department of Education.

La Voz Latina Hispanic Resource Center, Cincinnati, OH
Planned and taught reading to Latin Americans, ages 8-14.

EDUCATION_____

B.S. University of Cincinnati, May, 1992
Major: Elementary Education, GPA: 4.0
Minor: Spanish, GPA: 3.77
Endorsement: Junior High/Middle School, GPA: 4.0

HONORS AND ACTIVITIES_____

Volleyball Scholarship, Captain 1990
GTE Academic All-American
Eliza Baker Memorial Scholarship in Education
Fellowship of Christian Athletes
Kappa Delta Pi
Sigma Delta Pi, Secretary
Mortar Board
Phi Kappa Phi

INTERESTS_____

OASTI - Ohio Association of Science Teachers, Inc.
OCTM - Ohio Council of Teachers of Mathematics

SPECIAL SKILLS_____

TESA - Teacher Expectations and Student Achievement
CEI - Critical Elements of Instruction
Spanish fluency

REFERENCES AVAILABLE UPON REQUEST

PHILOSOPHY OF EDUCATION

Teaching in the 1990s is a growing profession. The nation is looking at ways to improve its educational system. Good teachers are at the heart of improving the nation's schools. I am enthusiastic that I have chosen teaching as my profession. I am looking forward to educating students of the 1990s and the next century.

As a teacher, I believe that all children are good. With positive guidance and positive learning experiences, children will display their best qualities. I feel that children learn through hands-on activities. With such experiences, children have the opportunity to actually participate in their learning rather than just listening to a teacher lecture.

I think it is important that classrooms are child-centered and geared toward the children's interests and attitudes. A child-centered classroom should reflect what is best for the children. When this happens, children feel like they are valuable to the teacher and the school.

A good teacher should like and respect children. Children need to feel they are good in the eyes of adults. These adults should allow children to participate in their learning and classroom experiences.

<pre>
                    Elizabeth R. Noble
                    221 Forest Drive
                    Iowa City, Iowa 52242
                    (319) 555 - 3546
</pre>

Objective   An entry-level position in elementary teaching
                which will allow me to utilize my technical,
                organizational, and interpersonal skills to
                assist young children to learn.

Education   Buena Vista College, Storm Lake, Iowa
                Department of Education
                Master of Science, Elementary Education 1991

                University of Iowa, Iowa City, Iowa
                Bachelor of Science Degree, Elementary
                Education 1989

                Chabot High School
                Graduate, May 1985

Experience   Research Assistant   January 1991 - Present
                Buena Vista College

                Researched several different motivation
                techniques on disabled readers who were
                reading two years below grade level.

                Education Program Staff   Summer 1989
                John W. Hereford Boys Clubs in Huntington, WV

                Designed, implemented, and evaluated
                recreational and educational programs for boys
                and girls, ages six through eighteen.

                Therapeutic Recreation Specialist Summer 1988

                Developed, implemented, and evaluated a
                comprehensive program of therapeutic,
                recreational, and cultural activities for one
                hundred plus developmentally disabled adults
                in a community-based day treatment program.

                Volunteer History

                Volunteered on a regular basis during
                college to work with children and adults
                through the following programs: Big
                Sisters/Big Brothers, Special Olympics,
                Tri-County Opportunity School, The Iowa
                Children's Museum, American Red Cross,
                Riverview Wellness Center, and Boys and Girls
                Clubs of America.

Training	TESA (Teacher Expectations and Student Achievement)
	Madeline Hunter's CEI (Critical Elements of Instruction)
	Cooperative learning, theory and application
	Whole language and thematic approach in the classroom
	Assertive discipline techniques

Skills	Computer Languages: FORTRAN, Pascal
	Computer Programs: WordPerfect, MacWrit/Write, Harvard Graphics
	Fluency in German

Activities	Senior class president
	Faculty Assembly Core Curriculum Committee
	Student Assembly representative
	Co-coach, Residential College women's team
	Spring sports spectacular
	Committee chairman of YMCA Giving Tree

Interests	Tennis, Soccer, Music

References	Available upon request

PHILOSOPHY OF EDUCATION

My philosophy of education has been developed from more than a decade of experience working with children. My strong philosophy and sincere affection for young people have inspired me to generously give of myself to ensure the highest possible output from each student. I look upon the success of my students as a reflection of my own performance. My approach can be summed up by one word -- POSITIVE!

Children learn best through positive experience. Understanding and retention are not fostered through the excessive use of workbooks and dittos but will flourish in an atmosphere of hands-on success. Children should be stimulated to take risks in the learning environment; creative expression and high levels of thinking should be encouraged. Teachers should not present themselves as omnipotent, but as people available at all times to provide guidance to students. To the greatest extent possible, I feel that classroom instruction should be individualized so that each student's needs are met. Children are in the classroom to learn, and educators should make the necessary adjustments to aid their students in achieving this goal.

A friendly, yet business-like classroom is important to a positive learning environment. Cooperative learning strategies encourage students to think for themselves, promote non-threatening competition, teach children to work together, and encourage the contributions of other students. Creating a variety of situations where students can experience educational and personal successes promotes positive attitudes toward learning which can carry through each student's educational career.

Parental involvement is important in shaping a child's attitude toward learning. Newsletters, periodic telephone updates, school programs, and conferences keep parents abreast of the progress of their child and encourage an active interest in that progress.

By writing and conducting stimulating lessons, teachers can foster a love for learning in their students. Relating subject matter to real life situations will focus students' attention on task and inspire a quest for additional knowledge. Integrated lessons reinforce prior learning and increase students' interest and retention.

It is imperative to stress to students that life is a continuing learning process. It is equally important to provide students with the tools necessary to answer their own questions after their formal education is complete. These are the critical differences between being taught, and being educated.

Maria P. Williams
3567 Hope Lane
Hanover, New Hampshire 03755
(603) 555 - 6786

OBJECTIVE:	To obtain a teaching position in elementary education.
EDUCATION:	B.S. Elementary Education Ball State University, Muncie, IN Graduation May 1992 Specialty Area: Kindergarten G.P.A. - 3.0 Major - 3.2
CERTIFICATES/LICENSES:	Elementary Education in Indiana (1 -8)
EMPLOYMENT HISTORY:	Wig's Catering May 1988 and May 1990 Loren P. Gordon (317) 555 - 1188 Responsibilities: Server Tabernacle Christian Academy June 1989 Mrs. Day (317) 555 - 8976 Responsibilities: Teacher Assistant Peter Rabbit Nursery 1985 - 1991 Mrs. Mary Boyd (317) 555 - 9821 Responsibilities: Volunteer, inspire young children, assist in special projects (food drives). Created an ongoing volunteer program involving St. Thomas High School Broad Ripple Park 1987 summer Kenn Williams (317) 555 - 0987 Responsibilities: Camp counselor 5 - 6 year olds.
ACTIVITIES AND HONORS:	Dean's List 1989, 1990, and 1991 Kappa Alpha Theta Sorority 1987 - 1991 Parliamentarian 1987 - 1989
INTERN EXPERIENCE:	Term 1 Forest Dale January 1991 - March 1991 Third Grade Marge Silvers (317) 555- 2245 Student Teacher Term 2 Christ the King March 1991 - May 1991 Kindergarten Mary Ellen Lipinski (317) 555 - 7765

PROFESSIONAL DEVELOPMENT:	Attended professional inservice seminars and workshops including: Assertive Discipline Gifted and Talented Introduction to Computers PFS Writer Word Processing Hemispheres of the brain Member of the Homer Carter Reading Council Title II Indiana Middle School Math Resource Teacher Project through KVISD
COMMUNITY:	Volunteer Librarian Room Mother Little League Concession Volunteer Drug and Alcohol Abuse Task Force

REFERENCES AVAILABLE ON REQUEST

PHILOSOPHY OF EDUCATION

I feel that my responsibility as a teacher is to educate children and develop their intelligence. A democratic society cannot survive without educated citizens and responsible, highly-trained leaders. Good citizens must be prepared with basic skills and much information which will enable them to think independently and to learn self-discipline.

As a teacher, I should provide for individual differences of ability. Each student should be challenged to reach the highest level of his/her mental, physical, and emotional ability. I would try to create an environment in the classroom where each child is equally valued and appreciated. Teaching should never humiliate or injure a child's self-esteem.

It is essential that standards be clearly defined and that discipline be firm, fair, and consistent. The methods of measuring achievement should be understood by students, parents, and school personnel. High expectations from a teacher will produce maximum results from the students.

I would hope that as a teacher I could encourage respect for learning and intellectual achievement by stimulating individual curiosity about the world and all of mankind. I want to help students acquire a knowledge of the fundamentals that will allow them to think logically, clearly and independently in order to prepare themselves for the future.

PATRICIA Q. TRAPP
1726 Willow Springs Walk
Blue Springs, MD 64015
(816) 555 - 9997

OBJECTIVE

To teach high school English

SUMMARY

I am a confident, outgoing individual looking for a challenging
and rewarding position. I enjoy interacting with others and
am involved in several athletic and religious groups. As an
avid distance runner, I train year-round and have competed in
the Boston Marathon.

EDUCATION

Purdue University; Lafayette, Indiana; Bachelor of Science,
Elementary Education; Kindergarten Endorsement; Graduation Date
May 1992.

PROFESSIONAL EXPERIENCE

Student Teaching. Brentwood Early Childhood Center,
kindergarten, Anderson, Indiana. April-May 1991.
Designed and implemented developmentally appropriate activities
for both morning and afternoon classes.

Student Teaching. Edgewood Elementary School, Grade 1, Anderson,
Indiana. January-March 1991.
Taught 15 mixed ability children using a variety of instructional
methods including cooperative learning and use of learning
centers. Planned several learning centers as well as
instructional games/aids. Planned and supervised a field trip.

Teaching Practicum. Meridian Hills Co-op Nursery School,
Indianapolis, Indiana. August-December 1990.
Designed and implemented developmentally appropriate activities
for 3-year-olds. Included opportunities for language development
as well as hands-on exploration of school environment.

Camp Counseling. Camp Indogan, Angola, Indiana. summers:
1986-present.
Taught crafts to sixty to eighty 9,10, and 11-year-olds.
counseled twelve girls, organized presentations of cabin skits.

Training. Elder-Beerman Department Store, Marion, Indiana. June
1988-present.
Assisted in training of new employees regarding operation of
customer service office.

Tutoring. Gas City, Jonesboro, Marion, Indiana. 1986-1990
Tutored elementary school students in all subject areas.
Specialized in increasing reading ability.

Literary Magazine Editor. English Department, Butler University,
Indianapolis, Indiana. Fall 1989 to present.

AWARDS

Dean's List 1990
Kappa Gamma Sorority Outstanding Member Scholarship

ACTIVITIES

House Manager Kappa Gamma
Volunteer for Gleanar's Food Bank
Glee club
YMCA

SKILLS

Desktop Publishing/Macintosh
Pagemaker
Hypercard
MS Word

CERTIFICATION

Indiana Secondary Education Teacher's Certification: Summer
1991

PHILOSOPHY OF EDUCATION

I believe that it is my responsibility to provide an environment in which my students can develop a sense of worth that will allow them to make real contributions to society. I feel that this can best be achieved through cooperative learning. When a student is encouraged to work with others to attain a common goal, he feels a part of the group and realizes the importance of his own opinions.

I feel that children should be taught to be good thinkers. Cognitive skills can be used in many ways throughout their lives. Learning seems to have much greater significance for students when they have been given the opportunity to discover on their own rather than having the information dictated to them by the teacher. This self-discovery inspires higher levels of thinking.

Everyone deserves an equal chance to learn in the classroom. Teachers should set high expectations for all of their students. Both the "high achievers" and "low achievers" should not be frustrated by expectations that are too high.

I truly believe that I have chosen the greatest profession of all. It is imperative that I strive for excellence at all times to inspire the same standards in my students. The students who enter my classroom have the potential to be good or bad so it is up to me to influence them in a positive way.

ALEXANDER HO

986 Parker Lane   Business (415) 555 - 2939
Walnut Creek, CA 94595   Home   (415) 555 - 9875

CAREER OBJECTIVE

Teach journalism at the high school level and advise yearbook and
newspaper productions.

EDUCATION

Butler University, Indianapolis, Indiana
Bachelor of Arts in Journalism, May 1992

Cumulative G.P.A.: 2.6/4.0 Scale

RELATED COURSES

Newswriting and Reporting
Public Relations Methods
Mass Communication Law
News Editing
Advanced Advertising Copywriting
Reporting Public Affairs
News Photography
Graphic and Typography

LICENSE

Licensed to teach journalism to grades 9 - 12 in Indiana. May
1991

PROFESSIONAL EXPERIENCE

Student Teacher at Arsenal Technical High School, Indianapolis,
Grades 9 -12, Spring 1991
Student Teacher at Ben David High School, Indianapolis, Grades
10 -12, Spring 1991
Substitute Teacher at four different high schools in Indiana,
1988 - 1989
Staff Reporter for The Butler Collegian newspaper, 1987-1988
Secretary for the Society of Professional Journalists, 1911
Editor of yearbook and newspaper at Culver High School, 1986 -
1987
Designed radio, newspaper, and billboard advertisements for
Carpet Outlet, Plymouth, IN

WORK EXPERIENCE

Irwin Library at Butler University   Student Assistant
Circulated library materials to students; Helped students with
the use of microfiche and microfilm equipment; Assisted with
transition from manual to automated card catalogue system;
Processed research works for professional bindery; Performed
opening and closing procedures. Indianapolis, IN 1987 - Present

Duke Associates [through Quality Temporaries]   Receptionist
Operated 14 incoming calls switchboard; Greeted executive clients
and performed customer relations; Assisted with secretarial
duties. Indianapolis, IN. Summer 1990.

Indiana Department of Natural Resources   Creel Surveyor
Surveyed fishermen on Lake Maxinkuckee in Indiana to gather
information for the DNR program to increase walleye population;
Promoted DNR programs by performing various public relations.
Culver, IN.   Summer 1989

AWARDS

Nominated for Hilton U. Brown Scholarship by Butler Journalism
Department, 1989
Keitzer Scholarship, 1987 - 1991; Indianapolis News "Most
Valuable Staffer," 1987

PERSONAL

Hobbies include: fishing, water-skiing, volleyball, flag
football, doll collecting

REFERENCES

Recommendations are available upon request. A credentials packet
is available from the Educational Placement Office, Butler
University, 4600 Sunset Ave., Indianapolis, IN 46208.

Faculty Data Summary Sheet

Risler, Margaret, Ph.D.
Professor of Education
Graduate and Undergraduate Faculty

1. Academic Degrees

   Ph.D.   Kansas State University   1980
   M.S.   University of Indiana   1969
   B.S.   Purdue University   1968

2. Professional Experience

   1988 - present   University of Cincinnati, Associate Professor
                    of Foundations of Education

   1984 - 1989   Butler University, Associate Professor of
                    Foundations of Education (on leave 1986-1988)

   1986 - 1988   U.S. Department of Education, Office of
                    Research, Director, Education and Society
                    Division

   1981 - 1984   University of South Carolina, Assistant
                    Professor of Foundations of Education

   1977 - 1981   Kansas State University, Assistant Professor
                    of Education

   1973 - 1977   Ohio Wesleyan University, Graduate Teaching
                    Assistant

   1971 - 1973   United State Armed Forces Institute,
                    Education Research Specialist

   1969 - 1971   Indianapolis Public Schools, Social Studies
                    Teacher

3. Faculty and Administrative Load

   Fall Semester, 1989
   EDUC 208   The School and the Community   3 semester units
   EDFN 408   Introduction to Reading   3 semester units

   Spring Semester, 1990
   EDUC 202   The School and the Community   3 semester units
   EDFN 748   The School in Modern Society   3 semester units

   Summer Semester, 1990
   EDFN 408   Introduction to Reading   3 semester units
   EDFN 748   The School in Modern Society   3 semester units

Other Collegiate Assignments, 1989 - 1990

Tenure and Promotion Study Committee (Department)
SACS Committee (Department)
Committee on Higher Order Thinking (College)
Families, Communities, and Children's Learning Center
Committee (University)

Advising: Six doctoral committees (major professor on
            two)

4. Current Professional and Academic Association Memberships

American Educational Research Association
American Educational Studies Association
Associates for Research on Private Education
Conference on Faith and History
History of Education Society
Midwest History of Education Society
National Council on Religion and Public Education
Southern History of Education Society

5. Current Professional Assignments and Activities

President Elect, Associates for Research on Private Education
AERA/SIG
Program Chairman, Religion and Education AERA/SIG
Guest Editor, Private School Monitor
Reviewer, Educational Foundations
Member, Editorial Board of Review for Religion and Public
Education
Proposal Reviewer, AERA/SIG Associates for Research on
Private Education Proposal Reviewer, AERA/SIG Religion
and Education
Consultant, U.S. Department of Education, Office of Research

6. Publications

Books

Risler, Margaret M.   How To Prepare For School, National
Textbook, 1990

Risler, Margaret M.   Ready For Kindergarten, National
Textbook, 1989

Risler, Margaret M.   Vocabulary for the Elementary
Student, National Textbook, 1988

Risler, Margaret M.   Get to School, McKinny Press, 1987

Articles

Indianapolis News. "Why Parent Should Read to Their Children Daily"

Cincinnati Enquirer. "Getting into College"

Free Time. "Books to Read to Help You Get Into College"

7. Research

How T.V. Hurts Children's Ability to Read.

Home Schooling

FACULTY DATA FOR VITA SUMMARY SHEET

AVARD LEWIS

Associate Professor of Library and Information Science
Graduate Faculty - Appointed 1988

1. Academic Degrees (degrees, institutions, dates, field of specialty)

BS	Purdue University	1963-1967	Education
MLS	Ball State University	1971-1972	Library Science
AMLS	Indiana University	1974-1975	Library Science
Ph.D.	Indiana University	1974-1976	Library Science

2. Professional Experience

8-76 to date	Associate Professor, School Library Media Program Coordinator, The USC
6-75 to 8-76	Instructor, School of Library Science, FSU
9-70 to 6-74	Head Librarian, Ashbrook Senior High School, Indianapolis, IN
9-67 to 6-70	Head Librarian, Purdue University
9-67 to 6-71	Assistant Librarian, Purdue University

3. Faculty and Administrative Load (Course Number, Complete Course Title, Number of Credits.)

Spring, 1990

LIBR	J711	Seminar in School Library Media Programs	3 Credits
LIBR	J709	Fdns. of Information Sources & Services	3 Credits
LIBR	764	Internship	
LIBR	752	Independent Study	

Fall, 1989

LIBR	720	Admin. of School Libr. Media Programs	3 Credits
LIBR	J709	Fdns. of Information Sources & Services	3 Credits
LIBR	764	Internship	
LIBR	752	Independent Study	

Summer, 1990

LIBR	741	Education Services in Libraries	3 Credits
LIBR	764	Internship	3 Credits
LIBR	752	Independent Study	3 Credits

Other Collegiate Assignments, 1989-90 (Committees, Number of Advisees)

Chairperson, Telecommunications Advisory Committee of the University.
Faculty Rep. on the National Assoc. for Teacher Education.
Faculty Rep. on the National Assoc. for State Depts. of Teacher Education and Certification. Reader for sponsored Programs & Research, Research & Productivity Awards. Education and Certification.
Reader for sponsored Programs & Research, Research & Productivity Awards.
Faculty Rep. from the College to the University Teacher Education Programs Committee, now called the Professional Education Participants Committee.

4. Current Professional and Academic Association Memberships (Asterisks indicate meetings attended.)

    * Library & Infomation Science Education Consortium
    * Association of Library & Information Science Education
    * SC Association of School Librarians.
    * Association for Library Service to Children
    * Library & Information Technology Association

5. Current Professional Assignments and Activities (Non-teaching includes consultant·work and advisory functions)

Editor, "School News," a monthly column related to research in school library media programs in School Library Media Activities Monthly. (1989-1990)

"Getting the Facts to the Parents." Homeschooling Journal. Spring 1988

Critical review of language arts textbooks aimed at grades 9-12 for library and information skills for World Book and National Textbook. February 1990. Honorarium.

Consultant, Richland Northeast High School, on international education Advise the International Center on University-community cooperation related to international education.

6. Publications
"Should a Child be Six Before Entering Kindergarten?" National Forum of Applied Educational Research Journal, in press.

"Get the Kids Organized." Educational Digest. September 1988

"Homework: The Evening Battle." Parent's Digest. August 1987.

7. Papers presented
    Homework: The Evening Battle.

    Rethinking Kindergarten. Presented at the Annual Meeting of
    the American Association of Colleges for Teacher Education,
    May 1986.

8. Research
    Additional studies on Kindergarten and parents attitudes to
    being six before starting. The data base for this research
    includes several thousand cases collected nationally.

    Research on children's perception of luck and the onset of
    probabilistic thinking.

Jessica Adams
121 Hawthorne Drive
Alameda, CA 94103
510-555-8520

Educational Background: B.A. Stanford University (1965)
M.A. in Education, Holy Names College (1968)

Additional Work: St. Mary's College; California State University,
Hayward; California State University, Chico; University of
California, Santa Cruz; University of Hawaii

Credentials:
Standard Elementary
Standard Designated Subject Secondary
General Secondary
General Pupil Personnel Services
Administrative
Specialist: Reading
Specialist: Learning Handicapped

Teaching Experience:
Castilleja School, grades 1-12 (1 year)
American School in Japan, grade 4 (3 years)
Carlmont High School (6 years)
San Jose District Summer School (2 years)

Coordination:
Santa Clara Valley Unified School District, reading volunteers
(1 year)
District Reading Committee (7 years)
District Special Education Committee (6 years)
Work Experience Coordinator, Carlmont High School (3 1/2 years)

Supervision:
Student aides, work experience (3 years)
CETA aide, career education, creation and formation
of the Valley Youth Employment Center (1 year)
Work Study Program, district level (3 1/2 years)
Summer school student aides, 4 to 6 programs (2 years)
Teaching aide, Master Plan (3 years)
Additional program and aide (1 year)
Lead teacher, language arts, Carlmont High School
(4 teachers in department)

Alexandra Clarke
85 Starmont Lane
Kalamazoo, MI 49002
(616) 555-6812

CAREER OBJECTIVE

A teaching position in an elementary classroom or in an elementary classroom for the mildly mentally handicapped

EDUCATION

Bachelor of Science, December 1991
Major: Elementary Education
Endorsement: Special Education (MIMH)
Ball State University, Muncie, Indiana

Grades: 3.302/4.0 (major), 3.85/4.0 (endorsement)
          3.49/4.0 (overall)
Honors: Kappa Delta Pi (Honor Society in Education)
          3/90-present, Dean's List (5 times), EXEL Program
NTE: Completed July 1991

PROFESSIONAL EXPERIENCE

1/91 - 4/91   Student Teacher, Longfellow Elementary School, Muncie, Indiana. Taught spelling, reading, math, handwriting, social studies, and language arts in a first grade classroom with sixteen students. Responsible for planning and teaching daily lessons.

WORK EXPERIENCE

6/91 - 8/91   Secretary, Kelly Services, Indianapolis, Indiana. Worked at Kraft Foodservice using Word Perfect 5.1 and performing other secretarial duties.

4/91 - 5/91   Substitute Teacher, Muncie Community Schools, Muncie, Indiana. Taught grades one through six in all subject areas.

8/88 - 12/90   Math Grader and Computer Lab Assistant, Ball State University, Muncie, Indiana. Graded math exams, loaded computers and helped students if they had problems with educational software.

ACTIVITIES AND INTERESTS

Volunteered for an autistic child using the Sun-Rise Program, 1/89 - 5/89.

Mary Colbert
428 Lowell Street
Santa Clara, CA 94502
209-555-8365

Objective	Position as a K-6 elementary teacher
Credential June 1990	<u>Multiple Subject</u> California State University, Hayward, Supplementary ESL Authorization
Education 1989	<u>M.A. in Linguistics</u> University of California, Davis
1988	<u>B.A. in Linguistics</u> Minor in Psychology University of California, Davis
Honors 1988	<u>Graduated with Honors</u> University of California, Davis
1985-1987	<u>Dean's·List</u> University of California, Davis

Employment Highlights
1989-1990 — <u>Student Teacher - Grades 1,3</u>

Sunset Elementary
285 Susan Drive
Livermore, CA 95490
Linda May, Master Teacher

Teach all subject areas
1. Multiethnic students
2. Literature-based reading
4. Oral language development
5. Project Learning Tree
6. Math lab

Carl Munck Elementary
110 Main Street
Oakland, CA 99461

Ardenwood Elementary
333 Amelia Lane
Fremont, CA 95364
Karen McCall, Master Teacher

Other Experiences
1988-1989 — <u>ESL Clinic Instructor</u>
1. Multiethnic ESL students
2. Design syllabi and provide instruction using ESL materials

University of California,
English Department
Davis, CA 96416

1987

West Davis Elementary
1271 Miller Road
Davis, CA 96416

Professional Activities
1989-Present

1990

Placement File

ESL Internship
1. Teach multiethnic ESL students
2. Pull-out format

CATESOL (California Association of Teachers of English to Speakers of Other Languages)

TESOL (Teachers of English to Speakers of Other Languages)

Career Planning and Placement Center, California State University, Hayward

Johanna Brown
133 Lincoln Dr.
Detroit, Michigan 48099
(613) 555-3361

POSITION DESIRED   Elementary or Middle School Classroom
                    Teacher

CERTIFICATION   Michigan Continuing Certificate
                    Grades K-8th All Subjects
                    Grades K-12th Reading

EDUCATION   Master of Arts Degree, April, 1972, Western
                    Michigan University, Teaching of Reading.
                    Bachelor of Arts Degree, April, 1968,
                    Western Michigan University.
                    Major: Social Science.
                    Minor: Elementary Education.

TEACHING
EXPERIENCE   1980-1987 Substitute Teacher for Vicksburg
                    Community Schools and other area districts.
                    Long-term replacement positions include
                    1st, 3rd, 7th, and 9th-12th grades.
                    Responsible for report cards.

                    1971-1972 Substitute teacher for Vicksburg,
                    Portage, and Schoolcraft School Districts.

                    1968-1971 2nd Grade Teacher, Plainwell
                    Community Schools, in a contained
                    classroom.

COMMUNITY
SERVICE   Volunteer Librarian, 3 years. Room Mother,
                    8 years. Girl Scout Leader, 1 year.
                    Member of the Committee to Introduce
                    Computers into the Vicksburg Schools.
                    Member of the Committee to Study the
                    Comcept of a Middle School in Vicksburg.

RELEVANT
INFORMATION   Participated in professional inservice
                    seminars such as: Assertive Discipline, Gifted
                    and Talented, Introduction to Computers, PFS
                    Writer Word Processing Workshop, The
                    Hemispheres of the Brain, Lynn Hall's lecture
                    relating Occupational Therapy to the
                    classroom. Member of the Homer Carter
                    Reading Council.

REFERENCES   Available upon request.

Evelyn Moore
4366 South Street
Detroit, Michigan 48062
(616) 555-9698

Career Goal: To obtain a position as a secondary
                 education instructor in the areas of
                 Mathematics and Computer Science.

Education: September, 1987 - Present

                 Western Michigan University, Kalamazoo,
                 Michigan 49008. Secondary Education
                 Curriculum, Mathematics Major, Computer
                 Science Minor.

                 September, 1983 - June, 1987

                 Littlefield Public School, Albert, Michigan
                 48076. Graduated salutatorian June, 1987.

Work
Experience: February, 1989 - Present

                 McDonalds. 39 King Drive, Detroit,
                 Michigan 48071. Phone (616) 555-5137. Swing
                 Manager. Duties: cash audits, deposits,
                 quality control of product, customer
                 problems, supervision of employees, employee
                 assignments, inventory and ordering supplies,
                 restaurant appearance, register operations
                 and associated paperwork.

                 May, 1991 - Present

                 Mathematics and Statistics Department of
                 Western Michigan University. Kalamazoo,
                 Michigan 49006. Phone (613) 555-4620.
                 Computer Operator. Duties: software
                 inventory and evaluation, programming,
                 entering and updating files, journal
                 photocopying, and article synopsis.

                 September, 1989 - April 1990

                 Computer Science Department of Western
                 Michigan University. Kalamazoo, Michigan
                 49006. Phone (613) 555-1244. Grader.
                 Duties: grading assignments and quizzes,
                 recording attendance for lecture periods, and
                 communicating attendance results to the
                 corresponding instructors.

References: Available upon request

Elizabeth Sherrill
238 Sunset Dr.
Kalamazoo, Michigan 49718
(613)-555-5553

EMPLOYMENT HISTORY:

1985-Present	Substitute teacher for Lakeview Public Schools and Comstock Public Schools for over 100 days, all levels K-12 including shop, home economics, reading, band, art, and drafting.
1979-1985	Woodlawn Nursery School. Teacher of three and four year old children. Responsibilities included development and execution of art, music, language skills, small and large motor activities, discipline, classroom management, orientation, open house, special programs, curriculum, parent conferences, and evaluation and report cards for each student.
1967-1971	Comstock Public Schools, Kalamazoo, Michigan. Sixth grade teacher at Comstock Middle School. Supervisor of student teacher. Team teaching. Developed science curriculum. P.T.A. teacher representative.
1961-1967	Michigan Bell Telephone Company, Kalamazoo, Michigan. Long distance telephone operator.

EDUCATION:

1979-1982	Western Michigan University, Kalamazoo, Michigan. Completed eighteen hours of graduate work toward Masters Degree in Elementary Education.
1967-1971	Western Michigan University, Kalamazoo, Michigan. Completed twenty hours of graduate credit for elementary certification.
1963-1967	Western Michigan University, Kalamazoo, Michigan. B.S. Degree in Secondary Education. Earth Science and History Majors.
1959-1963	St. Augustine High School, Kalamazoo, Michigan. Diploma 1963.

COMMUNITY SERVICE:

1976–Present   Girl Scout Leader, five years. Webelos,
                        one year. PTA, nine years. Hot lunch
                        volunteer, three years. Room mother, nine
                        years.

REFERENCES: Available upon request.

Stephanie Johnson
5024 Orinda Lane
Indianapolis, Indiana 64022
(317) 555-9601

GOAL: A teaching position for grades kindergarten
through third.

EDUCATION:
MARIAN COLLEGE
Indianapolis, Indiana
Bachelor of Science, 1985
Early Childhood Education Major
Dean's List: May, 1983 and December, 1983
GPA: 3.0 (A=4.0)

INDIANA UNIVERSITY
Bloomington, Indiana

EDUCATION-RELATED COURSES
Early Childhood Education
Early Childhood Guidance Practicum
Math Elementary School Teacher
Language Arts for Preschool
Curriculum Enrichment for Young Children
Curriculum Practicum
Movement and Health Experiences
Lab Experience: Kindergarten
Developmental Reading
Children's Theater
Children's Art
Corrective Reading
Introduction to Exceptional Children
Basic Science Skills
Children's Literature
Introduction to Music Fundamentals

EMPLOYMENT:
CHRIST THE KING CATHOLIC GRADE SCHOOL
8629 Weber Street
Indianapolis, Indiana 64022
Second Grade Teacher   1985-1987

POLLY PANDA CHILD CARE CENTER AND PRESCHOOL
Indianapolis, Indiana
Teacher
Nap Supervisor
Playground Supervisor   1983-1984

NORTHSIDE CHILD-FAMILY DEVELOPMENT CENTER
Indianapolis, Indiana Teacher
Nap Supervisor
Playground Supervisor
Secretary   1983

ACTIVITIES:
MARIAN COLLEGE
Student Affairs Committee
Play Performance

INDIANA UNIVERSITY
Intramural Softball
Dorm Hall Officer

CHATARD HIGH SCHOOL
Senior Class President
Student Council (four years)

INTERESTS:
Swimming
Bike riding
Singing
Poetry

REFERENCES:
Available Upon Request

LOUIS R. BECKLEY
3800 York Ave. South
Minneapolis, MN 55410
(612) 555-7908

OPEN TO RELOCATION

EDUCATION

BS, Butler University, Indianapolis, IN May 1991
Major: Elementary Education
Endorsement: Gifted and Talented

CAREER OBJECTIVE

I am seeking a position as an elementary school teacher with an
emphasis in a gifted and talented program. I hope to become part
of a child-centered school with a positive and progressive
environment which will allow me to grow professionally as an
educator. I am also interested in coaching swimming.

CERTIFICATES/LICENSES

Indiana Elementary Education Credential (1-8)
Indiana Gifted and Talented Endorsement

SPECIAL SKILLS

Trained in TESA (Teacher Expectations and Student Achievement)
and CEI (Critical Elements of Instruction)

ACTIVITIES and HONORS

Member of the Student Assembly
Member of Council on Presidential Affairs

REFERENCES

Furnished upon request...

Mark L. Longman
28 Limestone Drive
Springfield, Ohio 45501

CAREER OBJECTIVE: To obtain a teaching position in elementary education, preferably in primary grades, and to use my skills in an effective professional manner.

Education:

Western State College, Gunnison, Colorado. Bachelor of Arts Elementary Education, Special Area: Kindergarten
GPA 3.5/4.0

Employment:

Kiddy-Land 1985-1991
Responsibilities: Volunteer, inspire young children, assist in special projects (food drives) and create an ongoing volunteer program involving Lowell High School.

Gunnison Central Library 1983-1985
Circulated library materials to students; Helped students with the use of microfiche and microfilm equipment; Assisted with transition from manual to automated card catalogue system; Processed research works for professional bindery; Performed opening and closing procedures.

Computer Skills:

Knowledge of C and Pascal programming languages
Proficient in Word Perfect, Ventura Publisher, and Hotshot Graphics

Additional Information:

National Merit Scholar
Biked and traveled across Europe during the summer of 1990
Active member of the varsity swim team

REFERENCES: Available on request.

Anna Maria Houser
328 Pacific Heights
Chicago, IL 60646
(312) 555-8673

CAREER OBJECTIVE: Elementary School Teacher in the primary grades in a program that emphasizes science and mathematics.

EDUCATION: Northwestern University, Chicago, IL
Graduation date: May 1991
Bachelor of Science
Major: Elementary Education
Related Experience:
Student Teaching
Northview Elementary School, Glenview, IL
Fourth Grade, Open Concept
GPA 4.0

EMPLOYMENT HISTORY: Office Assistant. Elder-Beerman Department Store, Bloomington, IL. June 1990-present.
Responsible for training of new office employees as well as supervision of office operations. Occasional responsibility for compiling storewide payroll figures and daily monetary deposits.

PROFESSIONAL MEMBERSHIPS: International Reading Association, Chicago, Illinois Area Council of IRA.

SPECIAL SKILLS: Trained in TESA (Teacher Expectations and Student Achievement) and CEI (Critical Elements of Instruction).

ACTIVITIES AND HONORS: Paul Douglas Teacher Scholarship, Academic Scholarship, Dean's List, Outstanding Reading Student Award, Tau Beta Sigma Band Fraternity, Alpha Lambda Honor Society, Kappa Delta Pi International Honor Society in Education.

CERTIFICATES/LICENSES: Provisional Elementary License for grades 1-6, kindergarten endorsement expected May 1991.

Harry D. Lorton
196 Cambridge Drive
St. Paul, MN 55631
(612) 555 - 1213

OBJECTIVE: To obtain a teaching position in either elementary education or with children who have special needs in reading.

EDUCATION:

<u>University of Minnesota</u>, Minneapolis, MN
Currently in Master's program in Reading
<u>Syracuse University</u>, NY 9/83 - 5/86
Bachelor of Science
Major: Elementary Education
Minor: Reading

EXPERIENCE:

<u>Brentwood Elementary School</u>: January - March 1992
Marge Needham, Cooperating Teacher, Grade 5.
Student teaching responsibilities included: all teaching duties, attending staff and parent-teacher organization meetings, participating in textbook adoption sessions for social studies, attending Teacher In-Service Day to evaluate performance-based accreditation.

<u>Waterfront Director/Lifeguard</u>: Minnesota DNR, Saint Croix State Park: Stillwater, Minnesota - Summers 1987, 1988, 1989, 1990

<u>Public Relations Intern</u> - KFYI-TV Channel 2: Minneapolis, Minnesota
January until May 1990
Researched and wrote history of the station and assisted in public relations

<u>Literary Magazine Editor</u> - University of Minnesota: Minneapolis, Minnesota - Fall 1988 until present
Conducted staff meetings, selected published material, and designed the final layout

OTHER INFORMATION:

<u>Sigma Tau Delta English Honorary</u>

<u>John Newcombe Wright English Award</u>

<u>Pascal, Excel</u>

John Mitchell

Present Address: Permanent Address:
1324 Almond Street   223 Maple Drive
Bloomington, IN 47401   Carmel, IN 46032
(812) 555 - 9874   (317) 555 - 8975

OBJECTIVE   To secure a teaching position at the high school
level in the area of Language Arts

EDUCATION   Bridgeport College of Education, CT
Bachelor of Arts in English
June 1990

CERTIFICATION Indiana Secondary Education
Teacher's Certification: Summer 1991

EXPERIENCE   Child Care - September 1990 to present
Lawrence Kelsey
Indianapolis, Indiana

Public Relations Intern - Spring 1990
WFYI - TV Channel 20
Indianapolis, Indiana

SKILLS   Desktop Publishing/Macintosh
Pagemaker
Hypercard
MS Word

REFERENCES AVAILABLE UPON REQUEST

```
                         MICHAEL J. SCHULTZ
                         6225 Arlington Ave.
                         Mount Prospect, IL  60056
                         Home phone:   312-555-3366
                         Office phone: 312-555-9876
```

EDUCATION:

B.A. German (minor in Spanish), '71
Western Illinois University, Macomb, IL

M.A. in Educational Administration and
Supervision, '79
St. Xavier College
Chicago, IL

EXPERIENCE:
9/82-present

Assistant Registrar
I have been Assistant Registrar for
Registration at Roosevelt University in
Chicago, Illinois, since September 1982.

My primary duties are to supervise the entry
of the registration and biographic-
demographic data that is collected at
registration and to prepare and supervise
the registration processes. My staff and I
prepare the computer schedule to receive
registration data in order to produce class
cards, class lists, and grade rosters.
Also, I am responsible for production of the
class schedules and allocation of
classrooms. I have supervisory and payroll
responsibilities for 3 full-time and up to
50 part-time employees. I also have done
degree checks for students seeking
confirmation of progress toward their
degrees and athletic eligibility reports.

1971-1982

Teacher of Foreign Languages
Previous to holding the above position, I
taught German and Spanish on the secondary
level and in the adult education program at
Evergreen Park High School, Evergreen,
Illinois. I sponsored the German Club, was
active in curriculum planning workshops, and
chaired the screening committee for an
international student exchange program.

PROFESSIONAL
AFFILIATIONS:

Illinois Association of Collegiate
Registrars and Admissions Officers

REFERENCES:

Available upon request.

Rachel Allen Douglas
8965 Maple Dr.
Indianapolis, IN 46032
(317) 555-1876

EDUCATION

B.A. Spanish May, 1991
Western Illinois University, Macomb, Illinois

HONORS

Dean's List, Western Illinois University
Phi Delta Kappa, National Honorary in Education
Phi Beta Kappa
Recognition for Excellence in Teaching

PROFESSIONAL AFFILIATIONS

Midwest College Placement Association
Professional Development Committee
Newsletter Task Force
Liberal Arts Steering Committee

SUMMARY

I have worked at the university learning center. I tutored
students in Spanish and language arts. During my summer
vacations, I worked at Oakland Community College, Bloomfield
Hills, Michigan, as a clerk-typist. I was required to perform
various clerical duties such as typing and operating various
office machines.

INTERESTS

Exercising, reading, sewing, swimming, and tutoring children and
adults in Spanish and various other subjects.

CAREER OBJECTIVE

I am seeking a position as a high school Spanish teacher. I hope
to become part of a school that has a positive and progressive
environment which will allow me to grow as an educator. I am
also interested in coaching track and field.

PROFESSIONAL MEMBERSHIPS

Kappa Delta Pi

ANN MARIE FARRELL
625 N. 126 Street
Carmel, IN 46032
(317) 555-8765

EDUCATIONAL PREPARATION

Initial Principal's License, Post Graduate Studies in School of Administration, Purdue University, Lafayette, IN. Graduation from Experiential Program for Preparing School Principals (EPPSP) will take place in December of 1992.

Endorsement in Gifted Education, Purdue University, Lafayette, IN, 1989.

M.S., Education, Indiana University/Purdue University, Indianapolis, IN, 1978.

B.A., Elementary Education, St. Mary-of-the Woods, Terre Haute, IN, 1973.

PROFESSIONAL EXPERIENCE

1985-Present	Resource Teacher for Gifted/Talented Students (Grades 2-6), West Newton Elementary, Decatur Township, West Newton, IN.
1983-1985	Educator for Grades 4 and 5, Lynwood Elementary, Decatur Township, Indianapolis, IN.
1978-1983	Educator for Grades 5 and 6, St. Thomas Aquinas Grade School, Indianapolis, IN.
1973-1978	Educator for Grades 4 and 5, St. Peter's Grade School, Greenfield, IN.
October, 1973 March, 1974	Homebound Tutor for a student severely burned in an auto accident, New Palestine Indiana School System.

ADVANCED TRAINING AND SPECIAL ACTIVITIES

Learning Styles/Gregory Model, Indianapolis, Indiana.
Cooperative Learning, Indianapolis, Indiana.
TESA (Teacher Expectations and Student Achievement)

SONIA FERNANDEZ
5687 GREEN STREET
KALAMAZOO, MICHIGAN 90084
(616) 555-0987

PROFESSIONAL OBJECTIVE: TEACHING PRIMARY EDUCATION.

EDUCATION: BACHELOR OF SCIENCE, WESTERN MICHIGAN UNIVERSITY
                KALAMAZOO, MICHIGAN, DECEMBER 1989.

                ASSOCIATE OF ARTS, KALAMAZOO VALLEY COMMUNITY
                COLLEGE, KALAMAZOO, MICHIGAN, MAY 1985.

                MAJOR: ELEMENTARY EDUCATION
                MINORS: MATH/SCIENCE, ENGLISH

                CONSIDERABLE WORK IN TUTORING IN MATH,
                SCIENCE, READING, AND LANGUAGE ARTS.

EXPERIENCE:

1985-PRESENT   NC LEARNING CENTER, KALAMAZOO, MICHIGAN
                TUTORING STUDENTS IN PRE-KINDERGARTEN THROUGH
                EIGHTH GRADE IN SUBJECTS SUCH AS MATH, SCIENCE,
                READING, AND LANGUAGE ARTS.

1983-1985   DEPARTMENT OF SOCIAL SERVICES, KALAMAZOO, MICHIGAN
                FOSTER PARENT: KEEPING CHILDREN IN MY HOME.

1971-1983   EATON CORPORATION, KALAMAZOO, MICHIGAN
                BEGAN AS A CLERK-TYPIST IN THE TOOL DESIGN
                DEPARTMENT AND PROGRESSED THROUGH THE CLERICAL
                RANKS IN TOOL DESIGN, METHODS AND PROCESS
                ENGINEERING, ACCOUNTING, AND PAYROLL DEPARTMENT.

1970-1971   ALLIED ALUMINUM COMPANY, SOUTH BEND, INDIANA
                CLERK-TYPIST: KEEPING RECORDS ON PART NUMBERS
                (FENDERS, BUMPERS, AND BRAKES) AND TYPING INVOICES.

1969-1970   OAKLAND COMMUNITY COLLEGE, BLOOMFIELD HILLS,
                MICHIGAN
                CLERK-TYPIST: PERFORMING VARIOUS CLERICAL DUTIES
                SUCH AS TYPING, AND OPERATING VARIOUS OFFICE
                MACHINES.

INTERESTS: EXERCISING, READING, SEWING, SWIMMING, AND TUTORING

MARTHA CAMERON SMITH
68 MILLER ROAD
MINNEAPOLIS, MN 55401
(612) 555-9876

OBJECTIVE

TO OBTAIN A POSITION AS AN ELEMENTARY CLASSROOM TEACHER

CERTIFICATION

MICHIGAN PROVISIONAL CERTIFICATE
K-5 CLASSROOM
6-8 SCIENCE AND HEALTH

EDUCATION

BACHELOR OF SCIENCE, APRIL 1990
WESTERN MICHIGAN UNIVERSITY, KALAMAZOO, MI
MINORS: ELEMENTARY EDUCATION, SCIENCE AND HEALTH (CURRENTLY
ENROLLED IN MATH MINOR CLASSES)

INSTRUCTIONAL THEORY INTO PRACTICE: ITIP TRAINING, KVISD
(JUNE 1991)

RELATED EXPERIENCE

SUBSTITUTE TEACHING
PLAINWELL COMMUNITY SCHOOLS, PLAINWELL, MI
INDEPENDENTLY SUPERVISED UP TO THIRTY STUDENTS IN GRADES K-5.

DIRECTED TEACHING
INDIAN PRAIRIE ELEMENTARY SCHOOL, KALAMAZOO, MI
FIRST GRADE CLASSROOM. MANAGED CLASS INDEPENDENTLY ON A REGULAR
BASIS. ORGANIZED AND PRESENTED UNIT PLANS IN ALL SUBJECT AREAS
AND EXTENDED LESSONS WITH APPROPRIATE ACTIVITIES.
(JANUARY-APRIL 1990)

PARTICIPATION
GULL ROAD ELEMENTARY, COMSTOCK, MI
SECOND GRADE CLASSROOM. DIRECTED WHOLE GROUP INSTRUCTION AS WELL
AS INDIVIDUAL SMALL GROUP WORK IN MATH AND SCIENCE AREAS.
(SEPTEMBER-DECEMBER 1989)

NORTHEASTERN ELEMENTARY SCHOOL, KALAMAZOO, MI
FIRST GRADE CLASSROOM. ORGANIZED AND PRESENTED UNITS IN MATH,
SCIENCE AND READING SKILLS. DEVELOPED ENRICHMENT ACTIVITIES TO
SUPPLEMENT LESSONS. (JANUARY-APRIL 1989)
VOLUNTEERED TO REMAIN AS TEACHER'S AIDE. (APRIL-JUNE 1989)

OTHER EXPERIENCE

CERTIFIED BLOOD PRESSURE SCREENER, WMU WELLNESS CENTER (FEBRUARY 1988)
ASSISTANT MANAGER, MEDICAL TRANSCRIBER, SALES CLERK, AND ASSISTANT

REFERENCES AND CREDENTIALS

AVAILABLE FROM WESTERN MICHIGAN UNIVERSITY CAREER PLACEMENT SERVICES, KALAMAZOO, MI 46008.
(616) 555-2788

ROBERTA LARDNER

SCHOOL ADDRESS
8773 SOUTH 46TH ST.
INDIANAPOLIS, IN 46260
(317) 555-9876

PERMANENT ADDRESS
1159 CAREW DR.
INDIANAPOLIS, IN 46220
(317) 555-1177

JOB OBJECTIVE
SEEKING A SECONDARY MATH POSITION OFFERING INVOLVEMENT IN EXTRACURRICULAR ACTIVITIES.

EDUCATION
BUTLER UNIVERSITY, INDIANAPOLIS, IN   G.P.A. 3.3 ON 4.0 SCALE
DEGREE B.A. IN SECONDARY EDUCATION/MATHEMATICS, MAY 1991

SPECIAL SKILLS: EXTENSIVE COMPUTER TRAINING – KNOWLEDGE OF BASIC, FORTRAN, PASCAL, WORD PERFECT, AND MSDOS.

SECOND LANGUAGE – FRENCH

MOTIVATED, ORGANIZED, AND STRUCTURED. STIMULATED BY CHALLENGING SITUATIONS AND NUMERICAL ANALYSIS.

CAREER RELATED EXPERIENCE
SPRING 1991   NORTH CENTRAL HIGH SCHOOL   STUDENT TEACHER
                   TAUGHT UNITED STATES HISTORY
                   (REGULAR AND MODIFIED)

SPRING 1990   CHATARD HIGH SCHOOL   STUDENT TEACHER
                   TAUGHT ALGEBRA, TRIGONOMETRY, AND GENERAL MATH

FALL 1989   CHATARD HIGH SCHOOL, INDIANAPOLIS, IN
                   VOLUNTEER TEACHING ASSISTANT
                   FIELD EXPERIENCE: ASSISTED IN GEOMETRY AND
                   ALGEBRA COURSES IN THE SCHOOL'S MATHEMATICS
                   DEPARTMENT.

OTHER EXPERIENCE:
1988-1990   THE JOHNSON FAMILY, CARMEL, IN CAREGIVER AND HOUSE
            MANAGER
            RESPONSIBILITIES INCLUDED CARING FOR FOUR CHILDREN,
            PLANNING FAMILY ACTIVITIES, AND GENERAL HOUSE UPKEEP.

1987   DIANE McCOMBER SCHOOL OF DANCE GYMNASTICS INSTRUCTOR
            RESPONSIBILITIES INCLUDED TRAINING YOUNG DANCERS TO
            INTEGRATE GYMNASTICS INTO THEIR DANCING ROUTINES,
            SUPERVISING FIVE CLASSES OF 10-25 STUDENTS.

HONORS AND ACTIVITIES
Bowman Distribution Scholarship - $3,000 per year
Dean's Honors List - two terms
Phi Eta Sigma National College Honorary
Alpha Lambda Delta National College Honorary
Delta Gamma Fraternity - Pledge Class Officer and Assistant V.P.
Volunteer Work for Aid to the Blind
Lutheran Campus Ministry

REFERENCES
A closed file is available from the Director, Office of Academic
Program - Educational Placement, Butler University, 4600 Sunset
Avenue, Indianapolis, IN 46208. Telephone (317) 555-8877

MARIA PATRICIA GOODE

CURRENT ADDRESS
876 W. Hampton
Indianapolis, IN 46208
(317) 555-9174

PERMANENT ADDRESS
986 First Ave.
Ft. Lauderdale, FL 33041
(305) 555-8765

CAREER OBJECTIVE:

To obtain a teaching position in elementary education, preferably in primary grades, which uses my professional skills effectively.

EDUCATION:

B.S. Elementary Education Butler University; Graduation May 1991
Specialty Area: Kindergarten
G.P.A. - 3.0 Major - 3.2

CERTIFICATES/LICENSES:

Elementary Education in Indiana (1-8)

EMPLOYMENT HISTORY:

Jug's Catering May 1988 and May 1990
Responsibilities: Server

Tabernacle Christian Academy June 1989
Responsibilities: Playground supervisor

REFERENCES:

Charles White
35 Whispering Trees Lane
Fort Lauderdale, FL 33076
(305) 555-6643

Edward J. Fisher
1456 Burlington Avenue
Indianapolis, IN 46220
(317) 555-8904

LAURA R. WROBLEWSKI
3567 HOPE LANE
HANOVER, NEW HAMPSHIRE 03755
(603) 555 - 6786

CAREER OBJECTIVE_____

I AM SEEKING A POSITION AS AN ELEMENTARY SCHOOL TEACHER, WITH AN EMPHASIS IN A GIFTED AND TALENTED PROGRAM. I HOPE TO BECOME PART OF A CHILD-CENTERED SCHOOL WITH A POSITIVE AND PROGRESSIVE ENVIRONMENT WHICH WILL ALLOW ME TO GROW AS AN EDUCATOR. I AM ALSO INTERESTED IN COACHING TRACK AND FIELD.

EDUCATION_____

BUTLER UNIVERSITY, INDIANAPOLIS, IN, BS, MAY 1991
MAJOR: ELEMENTARY EDUCATION
ENDORSEMENT: GIFTED AND TALENTED

CERTIFICATES/LICENSES_____

SUBSTITUTE TEACHER'S LICENSE 12/89

SPECIAL SKILLS_____

TRAINED IN TESA (TEACHER EXPECTATIONS AND STUDENT ACHIEVEMENT) AND CEI (CRITICAL ELEMENTS OF INSTRUCTION)

WORK EXPERIENCE_____

TARGET, INDIANAPOLIS, IN. SALES ASSOCIATE (8/91 - PRESENT). RESPONSIBLE FOR WORKING WITH CUSTOMERS AND DEALING WITH THE PUBLIC.

BUTLER UNIVERSITY, MODERN LANGUAGE CENTER, INDIANAPOLIS, IN. STUDENT ASSISTANT (9/90 - PRESENT). RESPONSIBLE FOR USE OF FACILITY AND WORKING WITH MODERN LANGUAGE FACULTY, INCLUDING OPERATING AUDIO/VISUAL EQUIPMENT. EXPERIENCE WITH THE MACINTOSH SE, MICROSOFT WORD.

CHILD-CARE PROVIDER, JAN AND DICK DAY, INDIANAPOLIS, IN (7/89 - 5/90). RESPONSIBLE FOR TAKING CARE OF THEIR TWO CHILDREN.

UNDERGRADUATE AWARDS_____

DEAN'S LIST, FALL 1989, SPRING 1990, FALL 1990, SPRING 1991, FALL 1991; NAMED ONE OF BUTLER UNIVERSITY'S "OUTSTANDING STUDENTS," 1990, 1991; MORTAR BOARD; SPECIAL EDUCATION SCHOLARSHIP RECIPIENT.

UNDERGRADUATE ACTIVITIES_____

SENIOR CLASS PRESIDENT; FACULTY ASSEMBLY CORE CURRICULUM COMMITTEE; STUDENT ASSEMBLY REPRESENTATIVE; CO-COACH, RESIDENTIAL COLLEGE WOMEN'S TEAM, SPRING SPORTS SPECTACULAR; COORDINATOR AND TUTOR OF DIRECTION SPORTS TUTORING PROGRAM; SPRING WEEKEND COMMITTEE; FACULTY-STUDENT ROUND TABLE; SENIOR CHALLENGE COMMITTEE.

PROFESSIONAL MEMBERSHIPS_____

KAPPA DELTA PI

REFERENCES AVAILABLE UPON REQUEST

MARTHA K. BYE
22 VERA DRIVE
IOWA CITY, IOWA 52242
(319) 555 - 3546

OBJECTIVE   AN ENTRY-LEVEL POSITION IN ELEMENTARY LEVEL TEACHING
IN THE FIELD(S) OF REGULAR EDUCATION AND/OR LEARNING
DISABILITIES.

EDUCATION   BUENA VISTA COLLEGE, STORM LAKE, IOWA
BACHELOR OF SCIENCE, MAY 1990
MAJOR: ELEMENTARY EDUCATION
MINOR: LEARNING DISABILITIES

CHATARD HIGH SCHOOL
GRADUATE, MAY 1985

EXPERIENCE   RESEARCH ASSISTANT   JUNE 1991 - PRESENT
BUENA VISTA COLLEGE

SUBSTITUTE TEACHER   AUGUST 1990 - MAY 1991

SUBSTITUTED IN GRADE LEVELS K-12 AND ALL SUBJECT
AREAS.

STUDENT TEACHING
M.S.D. WARREN TOWNSHIP, BUENA VISTA, STORM LAKE,
IOWA

ACHIEVEMENTS   ALPHA SIGMA ALPHA SORORITY, SERVED AS SOCIAL
CHAIRMAN. CAMPUS CARNIVAL CHAIRMAN AND PRESIDENT.
RECEIVED THE RUBY EAST CROWN AWARD, 1991.
BIOCHEMICAL CLOTHE-A-CHILD CHAIRMAN OF IOWA.

FLUENCY IN GERMAN

INTERESTS   TENNIS, SOCCER, MUSIC

REFERENCES   AVAILABLE UPON REQUEST

James B. Anthony

5000 Rolling Hills Drive
Indianapolis, Indiana 46002

Education

Initial Principal's Certificate, Post-Graduate Studies, Butler University, Indianapolis, Indiana, Experiential Program for Preparing School Principals (EPPSP), 1991

Masters of Science, Secondary Education, Indiana University-Purdue University at Indianapolis, Indianapolis, Indiana, 1982

Bachelor of Arts, University of Evansville, Evansville, Indiana, 1976

Professional Experience

1991 - Present, Assistant Principal, Warren Central High School, Metropolitan School District of Warren Township, Indianapolis, Indiana

1981 - 1991, Secondary Classroom Teacher, Metropolitan School District of Warren Township, Indianapolis, Indiana

1977 - 1981, Secondary Classroom Teacher, Washington High School, Indianapolis Public Schools, Indianapolis, Indiana

1976 - 1977, Junior High Classroom Teacher, Pleasant View Junior High School, Richmond Community Schools, Richmond, Indiana

Honors

Nominated, WRTV-6 Teacher of the Week, Warren Central High School, 1990

Teacher of the Week, Warren Central High School, 1989

"Key to the City of Indianapolis," presented by Mayor William H. Hudnut III, 1985

Professional Affiliations

National Association of Secondary School Principals (NASSP)

Association for Supervision and Curriculum Development (ASCD)

Educational Achievements in Warren Township Schools

Leadership

> Helped redirect the educational vision and enhanced the educational climate at Warren Central High School

Curriculum

> Helped expand and develop curriculum through serving as a member of an Instructional Committee composed of faculty members, students, and parents.

Staff Development

> Helped implement a program of Goal Oriented Teacher Evaluation designed to improve instructors and instruction.

Presentations

L.I.F.E. Conference, School Law Update, Butler University, Indianapolis, Indiana

Schools for the 21st Century, Butler University, Indianapolis, Indiana

Anthony (2)

__Mentors__

Dr. James M. Smith, West Texas State University, Canyon, Texas

Mr. James Ellsberry, Butler University, Indianapolis, Indiana

Mr. Tim Armstrong, Associate Principal, Warren Central High School, Indianapolis, Indiana

Dr. Mike Copper, Principal, Columbus North High School, Columbus, Indiana

Mr. John Harris, Assistant Principal, Lawrence North High School, Indianapolis, Indiana

Anthony   (3)

LESLIE P. GISLER
3800 York Ave. South
Minneapolis, MN 55410
(612) 555-7908

OPEN TO RELOCATION

EDUCATION

BS, Butler University, Indianapolis, IN May 1991
Major: Elementary Education
Endorsement: Gifted and Talented

CAREER OBJECTIVE

I am seeking a position as an elementary school teacher, with an
emphasis in a gifted and talented program. I hope to become part of
a child-centered school with a positive and progressive environment
which will allow me to grow professionally as an educator. I am also
interested in coaching swimming.

CERTIFICATES/LICENSES

Responsible for the design and applications of product
components for automotive plastic body panels. This
includes recommending design changes and testing
product as to their reliability and durability.
As a project engineer I was involved in manufacturing
procedures, processing improvements, and trouble-shooting
production problems for tooling. I managed maintenance
activities and vendor contracts for production tooling.

SPECIAL SKILLS

Trained in TESA (Teacher Expectations and Student Achievement)
and CEI (Critical Elements of Instruction)

ACTIVITIES and HONORS

Member of the Student Assembly
Member of Council on Presidential Affairs

REFERENCES

Furnished upon request...

Maria Patricia White
28 Octavia Trace
Cincinnati, OH 45243
(513) 555-8673

CAREER OBJECTIVE: Safety Director, with specialization in compliance monitoring and disposal of hazardous materials.

EDUCATION: Northwestern University, Chicago, IL
Graduation date: May 1991
Bachelor of Science
Major: Elementary Education
Related Experience:
Student Teaching
Northview Elementary School, Carmel, IN
Fourth Grade, Open Concept
GPA 4.0

EMPLOYMENT HISTORY: Office Assistant. Elder-Beerman Department Store, Bloomington, IL. June 1990-present. Responsible for training of new office employees, as well as supervision of office operations. Occasional responsibility for compiling storewide payroll figures and daily monetary deposits.

PROFESSIONAL MEMBERSHIPS: International Reading Association, Cincinnati, Ohio Area Council of IRA.

SPECIAL SKILLS: Trained in TESA (Teacher Expectations and Student Achievement) and CEI (Critical Elements of Instruction).

ACTIVITIES AND HONORS: Paul Douglas Teacher Scholarship, Academic Scholarship, Dean's List, Outstanding Reading Student Award, Tau Beta Sigma Band Fraternity, Alpha Lambda Honor Society, Kappa Delta Pi International Honor Society in Education.

CERTIFICATES/LICENSES: Provisional Elementary License for grades 1-6/ kindergarten endorsement expected May 1991.

KERRY H. BOURNE
1732 Albana Drive
Indianapolis, IN 46200
317-555-5570

OBJECTIVE: To obtain a teaching position in an Elementary or Middle School.

TEACHING EXPERIENCE:

1988 - 1989   WISHARD MIDDLE SCHOOL, Taylor Mill, Kentucky
Mathematics/Language Arts Teacher

* Taught Algebra, English, and Creative Writing.
* Headed student government.
* Coached three cheer leading squads.
* Planned and operated fund raising projects.

1988 - Summer   NORTHERN UNIVERSITY, Highland Heights, Kentucky
Social Studies Teacher

* Developed enrichment program, "Travel The World."
* Taught gifted students, grades 4-8, Geography, Culture, and Language of foreign countries.

1986 - 1988   CARTHAGE ELEMENTARY SCHOOL, Edges, Kentucky
Fifth Grade Teacher
* Taught all subject areas to fifth grade classes.
* Coached cheer leading squad.

1985 - 1989   SULLIVAN LEARNING CENTER, Edgewood, Kentucky
* Math/Language Arts Teacher
* Instructed gifted and remedial students in areas of mathematics and reading

EDUCATION:

Mooreville College
B.A., Elementary Education, 1985
summa cum laude

Beckridge University
Seeking Master's Degree
Elementary Administration

REFERENCES FURNISHED UPON REQUEST

Shirley Erikson
1809 Maple Drive
Kalamazoo, Mi. 46302
614-555-9189

EDUCATION
B.A. Calvin College, Grand Rapids, Michigan
M.A. Michigan State University (reading)
related course work: 18 hours in mathematics education

PROFESSIONAL EXPERIENCE
1990-present - Instructor, Western Michigan University,
Math/Statistics

Educational Sales Consultant
Houghton Mifflin Company
School Division
Springfield, Illinois 50341

                                    November 1984-May 1990

Created inservices for customers in reading, mathematics,
language arts
Designed support materials for products
Consulted with teachers on building, individual needs or
problems.

Director Share Time Program
Reading and Mathematics
Grand Rapids Public Schools
Grand Rapids, Michigan 49305

                                    September 1980-June 1982

Interviewed/trained/evaluated staff positions
Managed budgets, payroll and scheduling
Provided inservice for instruction in schools in mathematics and
reading

Educator
Elementary Education
Grand Rapids Public Schools
Grand Rapids, Michigan 49305

                                September 1970-June 1980
                                September 1982-November 1984

Taught elementary grades 1st, 2nd, 4th, 5th
Designed and developed a mathematics laboratory, grades
pre-school through 5th grade, taught as lead teacher for two
years.
Organized district wide curriculum as mathematics consultant for
7 years
Created a metric awareness program for educators, business and
community
Managed curriculum textbook selection committee

Conference Chairperson
National Council Teachers of Mathematics
Brownsbury, Virginia

March 1988-March 1989

Coordinated planning of NCTM Regional Conference, Grand Rapids,
Maintained budget, supervised support chairs, organized program
booklet

Michigan Council Teachers of Mathematics
Kalamazoo, Michigan 49830   1974-present

Participated as regional director for four years
Reorganized constitution, by-laws, job descriptions, conference
guide
Served as President 1985
Organized Junior High Middle School Mathematics Competition
Systematized historical information as current Historian of
Organization
Set up conference facilitator position, held for three years

KRISTI CULLOM
2345 NORTH STATE AVENUE
INDIANAPOLIS, INDIANA 46345
HOME # (317) 555-5867

EDUCATION

Initial Principal's License, Post-Graduate Studies in School Administration, Butler University, Indianapolis, Indiana. Graduated December 1991 from the Experiential Program for Preparing School Principals (EPPSP).

Master of Education, Guidance and Counseling, Indiana University, Indianapolis, Indiana, 1985.

Bachelor of Science, Elementary Education, Ball State University, Muncie, Indiana, 1981.

**PROFESSIONAL
EXPERIENCE**

1986 to Date

ELEMENTARY SCHOOL COUNSELOR, Avon Community School Corporation, Indianapolis, Indiana.

Developed and implemented the Elementary Guidance Program in three elementary schools; Provides consultation to classroom teachers concerning behavioral, social, academic, and personal problems of students; develops classroom and individual discipline plans; presents classroom lessons; facilitates group counseling; participates in staffing and case conferences; participates on Teacher Assistance Team; handles child abuse cases; serves as a liaison for Child Protective Services and the school; organizes fifth grade Life Positive (Just Say No) Program in three buildings; creates and implements activities for Kindergarten through grade five classes to participate in during National Red Ribbon Week in three buildings; participates in scheduling; **serves as acting principal in principal's absence;** summer school experiences with grades 3 and 4; provides inservices to teachers; facilitates six week parenting workshops.

1985-1986	**TEACHER GRADE 6,** Brownsburg Community School Corporation, White Lick School, Brownsburg, Indiana.
1982-1984	**TEACHER GRADE 5,** Seton Catholic School, Richmond, Indiana.
1981-1982	**TEACHER GRADE 4,** Mississinawa Valley Middle School, Union City, Ohio.

**WORKSHOPS/
PRESENTATIONS**

"Parenting Skills Workshop," Parents at Avon Elementary Schools, Indianapolis, Indiana, 1990-1991.

"Team Building," Life Conference, Butler University, 1991.

"Effective Guidance Program for the Elementary School," EPPSP Cohort Group, Butler University, 1991.

"Alternative Schools," EPPSP Cohort Group, Butler University, 1990.

"School for the 21st Century," EPPSP Cohort Group, Butler University, 1990.

"Multicultural Education Curriculum in the Schools," EPPSP Cohort Group, Butler University, 1990.

"Goal Setting," White Oak and Maple Staff, Avon Elementary Schools, Indianapolis, Indiana, 1990.

"Love: The Healing Power," Indiana Association for Counseling and Development Annual Conference, Indianapolis, Indiana, 1989.

"Self Esteem Workshop," Staff at Day Nursery, Medical Center, Indianapolis, Indiana, 1989.

**PROFESSIONAL
AFFILIATIONS**

Association for Supervision and Curriculum Development.
Phi Delta Kappa.

REFERENCES

Available Upon Request

-2-

Marvin A. Marcato

101 Eagle Drive
Indianapolis, IN 46200
(555) 555-5555

Objective   To obtain an administrative position at the secondary level.

Education   **Butler University**, Indianapolis, IN
Experiential Program for Preparing School Principals
(EPPSP), December 1991
Major: School Principalship

Bowling Green State University, Bowling Green, OH
Master of Music, May 1989
Major: Music Education

Central Michigan University, Mt. Pleasant, MI
Bachelor of Music Education, May 1983
Major: Instrumental Music   Minor: Jazz Studies

Administrative Experience

1990 - Present   **Metropolitan School District of Decatur Township**, Indianapolis,
IN

Director of Secondary Summer School
Duties: Entire organization and implementation of secondary
summer school, grades 7-12, including: curriculum
development, teacher hiring and evaluation, student discipline,
ISTEP testing coordination, and general building operations.

Teaching Experience

8/87 - Present   **Metropolitan School District of Decatur Township**, Indianapolis,
IN

Director of Bands
Duties: Instrumental music director grades nine through
twelve; including concert, jazz, marching, and pep bands.
Music theory instructor.

7/86 - 8/87   **Avon Community Schools**, Indianapolis, IN

Band Director
Duties: Assist entire instrumental program, grades six
through twelve, high school jazz band director, and general
music grades six and seven.

Marcato (2)

8/85 - 7/86   **Bowling Green State University**, Bowling Green, OH

Graduate Assistant/Music Director
Duties: Responsible for organization and implementation of University Lab School.

6/83 - 8/85   **Tri-County Area Schools**, Howard MI

Director of Bands
Duties: Entire instrumental music program, grades six through twelve, and high school choir.

Professional Memberships

Association for Supervision and Curriculum Development (ASCD)
Indiana Bandmasters Association (State Officer)
Indiana State School Music Association

James S. Michaelson Ph. D.
3333 Elizabeth Street
Local, Indiana 47000

Home: (317) 555-3364
Office: (317) 555-9274

Educational And Professional Training

Doctor of Philosophy, Educational Leadership, Miami University, Oxford, Ohio 1988

Post-Graduate Studies, Guidance and Counseling, Xavier University, Cincinnati, Ohio 1981-1983

Master of Education, Public School Administration, Xavier University, Cincinnati, Ohio 1981

Bachelor of Science, Elementary Education, Miami University, Oxford, Ohio 1979

Professional Experience

<u>Superintendent</u>, Local School Corporation, Local, Indiana, 1988 - Present
Provided overall leadership and direction for a growing suburban school district in Central Indiana. Specific accomplishments include revamping the overall K-12 curriculum, building two modern elementary schools, increasing teaching salaries by 17 percent, and successfully negotiating of two labor contracts.

<u>Teaching Fellow/Adjunct Faculty Member</u>, Department of Educational Leadership, Miami University, Oxford, Ohio, 1986 - 1988
Taught undergraduate courses in the field of educational leadership, teacher education, and supervised student teachers in the area of elementary education. Served as an off-campus graduate instructor (Wilmington College) in the area of educational leadership.

<u>Elementary Principal</u>, North Union Local Schools, Richwood, Ohio, 1984 - 1986
Provided leadership for the overall operation of a multidimensional elementary school (K-6) with 500 students and 36 faculty members. Established a comprehensive microcomputer system for classroom usage. Developed long range planning, budgeting, and student scheduling initiatives.

<u>Assistant Elementary Principal</u>, Fairfield City Schools,
Fairfield, Ohio, 1982 - 1984

> Assisted with all areas of staff development, faculty evaluation, student discipline, and curricular innovation for a (K-5) elementary building of 800 students and 49 staff members. Directed and implemented a series of community relations projects.

<u>Classroom Teacher</u>, Fairfield City Schools,
Fairfield, Ohio, 1979 - 1982

> Introduced grade appropriate material (4-8) through oral presentations, visual demonstrations, and other innovative resources. Served as chairperson for numerous curricular design committees.

Denise R. Jacobson
9270 Harvard Drive, Apartment A
Indianapolis, Indiana 46000
(317) 555-7979

Career Objective

A challenging position in administration which will utilize my organizational, leadership, and interpersonal skills in a middle/secondary school environment.

Education

Member of the Experiential Program for Preparing School Principals (Cohort Group 9) at Butler University, Indianapolis, Indiana. Expected completion date December 1991.

Master's Degree in Secondary Education from Indiana University-Purdue University in Indianapolis, Indiana. Degree received May 1988.

Bachelor of Arts Degree from Hanover College in Hanover, Indiana. Graduate cum laude in May 1982.

High School Diploma from South Ripley High School in Versailles, Indiana. Graduated with honors in May 1978.

Professional Experience

Presently teaching secondary mathematics at Lawrence North High School in Indianapolis, Indiana.

Taught evening mathematics classes at Indiana Vocational Technical College in Indianapolis, Indiana.

Taught secondary mathematics and basic programming courses at Triton Central High School in Fairland, Indiana.

Extracurricular Responsibilities

Member of the Performance Based Accreditation Steering Committee at Lawrence North High School.

Committee member for the School Improvement Program #4 at Lawrence North High School.

Member of the Lawrence Education Association Discussion Team for the previous three years.

Mentor for a beginning teacher during the 1990-1991 school year at Lawrence North High School.

Student Council co-sponsor for the past four years.

Resume
of
Pamela S. Woods
1610 Willow Lane
New Haven, OH 57220

POSITION DESIRED: School Psychologist

PERSONAL: Born 3/16/51, married, 2 children

EDUCATION: North Salem University - B.A., Psychology
                       (1974)

                       Bellaire University - M.A., Psychology
                       (1982)

                       Williamshire University - Ed.S., School
                       Psychology (1991)

CERTIFICATION: School Psychologist I

WORK EXPERIENCE:

6/90 - 8/91   **Williamshire University Counseling & Testing
                       Clinic/Dept.**
                       Position: Graduate Assistant (20 hrs./wk)

4/87 - 3/90   **Kramer Clinic**
                       Position: Addictions Counselor

12/83 - 4/87   **Children's Services**
                       Position: Counselor

11/78 - 12/83   **Comp-tek, Inc.**
                       Position: Office Manager

OFFICES HELD/
MEMBERSHIPS: Williamshire University Graduate Council,
                            Student Representative

                       Association of Graduate Counselors at
                            Williamshire University, Vice President

                       National Association of School Psychologists,
                            Member

                       American Psychological Association, Member

REFERENCES: Furnished upon request.

ANGELA M. LORENZ
815 N. Campbell Ave.
Indianapolis, Indiana 46000
Home Phone: 317-555-4650
Work Phone: 317-555-5237

EDUCATIONAL PREPARATION

Initial Principal's License, Post Graduate Studies in School of Administration, Butler University, Indianapolis, Indiana. Graduation from Experiential Program for Preparing School Principals (EPPSP) will take place in December of 1991.
Endorsement in Gifted Education, Purdue University, Lafayette, Indiana, 1989.
M.S., Education, Indiana University/Purdue University, Indianapolis, Indiana, 1978.
B.A., Elementary Education, St. Mary-of-the-Wood, Terre Haute, Indiana, 1973.

PROFESSIONAL EXPERIENCE

1985-Present	**Resource Teacher for Gifted/Talented Students for Grades 2 and 3**, West Newton Elementary, Decatur Township, West Newton, Indiana.
1983 - 1985	**Educator for Grades 4 and 5,** Lynwood Elementary, Decatur Township, Indianapolis, Indiana.
1978 - 1983	**Educator for Grades 5 and 6,** St. Thomas Aquinas Grade School, Indianapolis, Indiana.
1973 - 1978	**Educator for Grades 4 and 5,** St. Michael's Grade School, Greenfield, Indiana.
Oct. 1973 - Mar.1974	**Homebound Tutor** for a severely handicapped student in Indianapolis School System.

ADVANCED TRAINING AND SPECIAL ACTIVITIES

Learning Styles/Gregoric Model, Indianapolis, Indiana.
Cooperative Learning, Indianapolis, Indiana.
TESA (Teacher Expectation/Student Achievement)
Clinical Supervision Training, Curriculum & Instruction Department, Decatur Township.
Critical Elements of Instruction (CEI - Madeline Hunter's Mastery Teaching Model)
TESA/CEI link with Butler University. Coordinated Site Based Evaluation through Department of Education for Gifted and Talented Program in Decatur Township.
Writing of Gifted and Talented Grant and Budget Participated in selection process of an administrator for the School of Education at Butler University.
Climate Audit Sanders Elementary, Indianapolis, Indiana.
Writing of Social Studies Curriculum and Policy Handbook Development Involved in building level training for **Outcome Based Education,** including site visit to Johnson City, New York.
Technology, School Improvement, Human Relations.

PROFESSIONAL AFFILIATIONS

Association for Supervision and Curriculum Development.
Currently applying for membership in Phi Delta Kappa through Butler University.
Currently applying for associate membership in Indiana Association of Elementary and Middle School Principals
Indiana Association for Gifted.
Member of School Board for Holy Cross Central School.

INTERESTS

Membership in a Woman's Book Club
Hiking
Traveling with my husband
Enjoy the fine arts

REFERENCES

Dr. James Smith, Director/EPPSP
Butler University
4600 Sunset Avenue
Indianapolis, Indiana 46220.
317 555-9274

Mr. Jim Ellsberry, Associate Director/EPPSP
Butler University
4600 Sunset Avenue
Indianapolis, Indiana 46220.
317 555-9774.

Mrs. Janet B. Larch
Principal, West Newton Elementary
7529 Mooresville Road
West Newton, Indiana
317 555-5237.

JACALYN ELAINE LYNN
1560 Bayswater Lane
Cicero, Alaska 46911
Home (731) 555-3104
Office (731 555-6067

CAREER OBJECTIVE

Administrative position that provides opportunity for
promotion, and offers experiences enhancing leadership and
intellectual development.

CAREER GOALS

Service and leadership within the schools of our youth.
Dedication to the pursuit of life-long learning.

EXPERIENCE

Administrative

Carmel Clay Schools
Carmel, Alaska
August 1991 - Present
Director of Education - Arbor Hospital

Develop and construct the curriculum of a 1-12 school
graded program. Implement treatment plan objectives of
students placed in an inpatient acute care psychiatric
facility. Organize and write the day school program
serving outpatient Special Education adolescents.
Re-direct the educational vision established by the
previous hospital (private sector) staff. Hire,
supervise and evaluate the initial Carmel-Clay staff.
Design and implement all procedures and operations.
Provide staff orientation, and professional development.
Establish the annual budget. Oversee daily operations.
Communicate with professionals, home schools, parents,
hospital staff and community members. Serve the
educational needs of 650 inpatient students and 15 day
school students annually.

Instructional

Carmel Clay Schools
Carmel, Alaska
August 1990 - June 1991
Psychiatric Day Program Teacher - Arbor Hospital

Provide an academic and affective educational program for severely emotionally handicapped students, while interfacing with all medical and therapeutic staff. Testing and creation of Individual Education Plans (I.E.P.s). Supervise students' transitional return to his/her home school and follow-up.

Eagle-Union Consolidated School Corporation
Zionsville, Nevada
August 1983 - January 1987, August 1989 - May 1990
Resource Teacher

Screen, evaluate and assess the educational needs of children suspected of learning disabilities, mild mental retardation, and/or emotional impairment. Create I.E.P.s and provide prescriptive instruction.

Wayne Township School Corporation
Indian Hills, Indiana
March 1983 - May 1983
Learning Disabilities/Intermediate Classroom Teacher

Provide instruction and learning experience for children diagnosed with learning disabilities in a self-contained classroom setting. Administer diagnostic evaluation, and create I.E.P.s.

Howard County Board of Education
Columbia, Pennsylvania
September 1980 - January 1983
Diagnostic/Prescriptive Teacher

Evaluate all referred students that were suspected of having learning disabilities, mental retardation, or emotional needs. Chair the local admission, review and dismissal school committee for the county special education department. Create I.E.P.s and annually re-evaluate students placed in special education programs. Assist the school psychologist in establishing the level of student need in placement/thus determining calculated hours of instruction. Instruct children placed in special education.

Logansport Community School Corporation
Logansport, Mississippi
September 1978 - June 1979
Resource/Diagnostic Teacher

Evaluate all referred students suspected to be in need of special education. Assist the school psychologist in

Jacalyn E. Lynn

special education placement, and construct I.E.P.s. Develop and provide educational experiences for children found to be in need of service.

Kokomo-Center Consolidated School Corporation
Kokomo, Illinois
September 1977 - June 1978
Profound/Multi-Handicapped Intermediate Classroom Teacher

Supervise assistants, and oversee daily physical therapy, sensory stimulation, feeding, care and nurturing of students. Assist in the transportation, ancillary classes, and ambulation of students.

Indianapolis Public Schools
Indian Hills, Indiana
September 1974 - June 1976
Moderately Retarded/Intermediate Classroom Teacher

Provide education and developmental tasks meeting the growth need of moderately retarded students. Lead these students in ancillary classes, and assist in Special Olympics. Supervise and devise the structure and activities of a teaching assistant. Participate in the local school unit committees. Evaluate student growth and create I.E.P.s.

Business

L.A. Connection, Incorporated
Carmel, Alaska
October 1986 - July 1989
Partner- Stockholder, President - Treasurer

Maintain the corporate records, establish the annual budget, prepare and implement all financial and accounting records. Supervise personnel, over-see the facility and maintenance. Establish sales/marketing strategies, set advertising, complete purchasing and inventory. Prepare the 5 year business plan, manage the construction and expansion into a new facility. Trademark the corporate logo, manage Workout Wear and L.A. Connection Workout and Training Centre.

WORKSHOPS AND PRESENTATIONS

Teacher Fever, Eagle Union Schools, Zionsville, Nevada 1989.

Alternative Schools, Butler University, EPPSP, Indian Hills, Indiana, 1990.

Jacalyn E. Lynn
-3-

Multicultural Education, Butler University, EPPSP, Indian Hills, Indiana, 1990.

Inpatient Education Model, Arbor Hospital, Indian Hills, Indiana, 1990 - 1991.

Schools of the 21st Century, Butler University, EPPSP, Indian Hills, Indiana, 1991.

In - Basket Problem Solving, LIFE Conference, Butler University, Indian Hills, Indiana, 1991.

Teaching the Severely Emotionally Handicapped Student, Carmel Clay Schools, Carmel, Alaska, 1991.

The Hospital Model, Carmel Junior High School, Carmel, Alaska, 1991.

Day Treatment in the Public School, Marion County Mental Health Association, Indian Hills, Indiana, 1991.

Day Treatment in the Public School, Madison County Mental Health Association, Anderson, Vermont, 1991.

EDUCATIONAL PREPARATION

Certificate, Initial Principal's License, Post-Graduate Studies in School Administration, Butler University, Indian Hills, Indiana, Graduated December, 1991 from the Experiential Program for Preparing School Principals (EPPSP).

Post - Graduate Studies in Computer Programming and Literacy, The Johns Hopkins University, Baltimore, Maryland, 1982.

Master of Education, Elementary Education/Special Education (Learning Disabilities - L.D., Emotional Handicaps - E.H., and Mental Retardation - M.R.), Butler University, Indian Hills, Indiana, 1976.

Bachelor of Arts, Elementary Education/Special Education (L.D., E.H., and M.R.), Purdue University, West Lafayette, Indiana,1974.

PROFESSIONAL ORGANIZATION MEMBERSHIPS

Indiana Council for Administrators of Special Education

Jacalyn E. Lynn
-4-

Association for Supervision and Curriculum Development

Phi Delta Kappa (educational honor society)

Council for Exceptional Children

MENTORS

Thomas Doyle - Assistant Director of Special Education
Hamilton - Boone - Madison Special Services Cooperative
Carmel Clay Schools
5201 East 131st Street
Carmel, Alaska 46034
(713) 555-9961

Jim Ellsberry - Assistant Director of the
Experiential Program for Preparing School Principals
Director of the
Indiana Principal's Leadership Academy
Butler University
4600 Sunset Avenue
Indian Hills, Indiana 46208
(137) 555-9274

Tom Ryan - Director of Special Education
Hamilton - Boone - Madison Special Services Cooperative
Carmel Clay Schools
5201 East 131st Street
Carmel, Alaska 46034
(713) 555-9961

Jacalyn E. Lynn
-5-

BRYCE T. STEWART

PERMANENT ADDRESS
8664 Clay Center Rd.
Carmel, IN 46032

CAMPUS ADDRESS
626 E. Seminary St.
Greencastle, IN 46135

OBJECTIVE
An elementary teaching position, grades 1-5.

EDUCATION
DePauw University, Greencastle, IN
Bachelor of Arts Degree in Elementary Education, May 1989
Minor in American History
GPA 3.52/4.0
Karl Marx University, Budapest, Hungary (December 1987)
Austro-American Institute, Vienna, Austria (Fall 1987)

EXPERIENCE
Student Teacher
Supervised learning activities for 34 fifth grade students:
-developed and implemented learning centers and resource areas
-designed problem solving environment for mathematics
-executed disciplinary procedures and held conferences with parents
-provided social studies instruction for 25 sixth grade and 27
fourth grade students
Central Elementary School, Greencastle, IN (Fall 1988)

Teaching Intern
Observed and aided activities for 24 fourth grade students:
-provided individual instruction in developmental math for 15
students
-instructed computer keyboard
-directed drama presentation
Orchard Park Elementary School, Carmel, IN (January 1988)

Teaching Intern
Aided fifth grade classroom of 18 gifted/talented students:
-instructed German language
-provided motivational strategies for independent learning
-monitored progress of student-designed reading curriculums
-implemented Bloom's taxonomy in social studies activities
Hinkle Creek Elementary School, Gifted and Talented Program,
Noblesville, IN (January 1987)

Camp Counselor
Served as head counselor:
-supervised 18 boys (ages 7-11)
-delegated responsibility to four counselors
-corresponded frequently with parents
-coordinated small and large group instruction in sailing, soccer,
swimming, riding, and lacrosse
Camp Lincoln for Boys, Lake Hubert, MN (Summers 1986-88)

ACTIVITIES
Delta Upsilon: Executive Board, 1988
Chapter Secretary, 1988
Social Chairman, 1987
Philanthropy Chairman, 1986
Ambassador Club: Steering Committee, 1986-87
DePauw Admissions Office: Tour Guide, 1986-Present
DePauw Orientation Leader, 1987
Intramural Sports, 1985-present

HONORS
Dean's List, 1986-present
Mortar Board (Senior Scholastic Society)
Kappa Delta Pi (Education Honor Society)

REFERENCES AVAILABLE UPON REQUEST

SUE PARK
7788 OAKDALE DRIVE
Youngstown, Ohio 45715
HOME (333) 555-1234
WORK (333) 555-4321

WORK EXPERIENCE

1985 - Present
    Sunshine Elementary School,
4455 Children Road
Cincinnati, Ohio 45899
Fifth-Grade Math and Reading Teacher.

1975 - 1985
    Alexandria Elementary School,
3398 Dog Leg Road
Trenton, New Jersey 34443
Sixth-Grade Math Teacher.

SUPPLEMENTARY WORK EXPERIENCE

Present
    Excelsior Grade Book Computer Consultant.

Present
    Working with George University as a supervising teacher for reading endorsement candidates and beginning elementary education students.

1985 - Present
    Junior Achievement Business Advisor.

1991 (Summer)
    Internship as Assistant Principal for Summer School.

1990 - 1991
    Served as a mentor for a first year teacher.

1989 - 1990
    Student Teacher Supervisor.

Supplementary work cont.

1986 - 1988	Elementary Mathematics Department Chairperson. Prepared reports and presentations for the school board on current math progress in our school corporation. Initiated, organized, and provided leadership for corporation-wide math meetings and workshops.
1987 & 1988 (Summer)	Sunshine Middle School, Elementary Summer School Teacher.
1980 - 1986 (Summer)	Henrietta School Corporation, Driver's Education Instructor.
1975 - 1980	Elementary Intramural Co-director.

EDUCATION

Jan. 1990-Dec. 1991	Initial Principal's License, Post Graduate Studies in School Administration, Butler University, Indianapolis, Indiana. Graduated December, 1991 from the Experiential Program for Preparing School Principals (EPPSP).
1977 - 1979	George University, Master of Science Degree in Education.
1971 - 1975	Henry State University, Bachelor of Science.

REFERENCES

Available upon request.

PERSONAL AND PROFESSIONAL RESUME OF
DAVID T. WILLIAMS

David T. Williams
3000 West Street
Anderson, Indiana 46000
Telephone: (317) 555-4444

Education

Ball State University, 9/65 - 11/69, Bachelor of Science, Music Education

University of Portland, 9/72 - 5/74, Masters of Music Education, Music Education

Butler University, 1/90 - 12/91, Post-Graduate Studies in Educational Administration, Principal's Certification

Work Experience Data

WHUT/WLHN Radio, Anderson, Indiana, 9/88 - Present
Duties: Control room operator, disk jockey, announcer, trainer for new personnel. (Part time employment)

WHBU Radio, Anderson, Indiana, 11/84 - 9/88
Duties: Control room operator, disk jockey, announcer for both studio and remote broadcasts, producer of commercials for advertising clients, trainer of new personnel. (Part time employment)

South Side Middle School, Anderson, Indiana, 8/74 - Present

Duties: Director of Instrumental Music. Department Head. Teach Band, Orchestra, and General Music to 7th, 8th, and 9th graders. Aid in the consolidation of two schools into one and transformation from 7-9 to 7-8 grades. Recruit for Beginning Band and Orchestra. Establish and maintain a feeder program for Madison Heights High School. Assist with the Madison Heights music programs throughout the year. Organize and host annual ISSMA Band/Choir/Orchestra Contest. Chairman School Wide Discipline Policy Committee. Substitute Assistant Principal.

Madison Heights High School, Anderson, Indiana, 8/74 - 8/89

Duties: Assistant Director of Bands/Band Director. Assist in all aspects of the high school program including the following areas: stage/jazz band, theory, marching band, concert band, orchestra, fund raising, uniform design and selection, building design, trip planning, programming. Establish a feeder program at the middle school while consolidating two schools into one.

Fred Meyer, Inc., Portland, Oregon, 9/72 - 7/74

Duties: Clerk in the automotive parts department. This job helped pay way through Graduate School at the University of Portland.

Westfield Washington High School, Westfield, Indiana, 8/70 - 6/72

Duties: Director of Music. Teaching all instrumental, vocal, and general music classes. Director of Beginning, Intermediate, and Advanced Bands. Director of Stage Band and Marching Band. Establish feeder program for the high school band. Teach private lessons.

Marion High School, Marion, Indiana, 6/70 - 7/70

Duties: Director of Summer Band program.

<u>Eastern High School, Greentown, Indiana, 11/69 - 6/70</u>

Duties: Assistant Director of Bands. Teach Beginning and Intermediate Bands. Assist with the high school band and stage band. Assist with the choir. Direct the instrumental music for the musical. Teach private lessons for brass instruments. Direct small ensembles.

Additional Experience

- Member of the Indiana State School Music Association State Board from 1986 to present.
- Vice-President of ISSMA 1987-1988.
- ISSMA Executive Board 1989-1990.
- Member of Screening/Interviewing/Hiring Committee for ISSMA Director 1991.
- Member of church choir. Active participation on church committees.
- Have performed in community theater presentation, both on stage and in the pit bands.
- Have sung with various community groups.
- Active in Community Concert Association.
- Member North Central Association Steering Committee and have participated in six evaluation teams.
- Assistant to the Director of Bands at the University of Portland 1973-1974. Duties included directing the Band, conducting small ensemble rehearsals, leading sectional rehearsals, directing the Jazz Ensemble teaching Brass Methods classes.
- Assistant to the Choral Director at the University of Portland 1973-1974. Duties included directing rehearsals.
- Counselor at the Mid-American Music Camp. Regularly hired as guest conductor, clinician, and adjudicator.

RESUME OF QUALIFICATIONS
OF
PATRICIA WHITE
987 W. 44th St.
Cheyenne, WY 82001
(307) 555-9872

PROFESSIONAL OBJECTIVE

Opportunity to demonstrate superior teaching ability and administrative decision making skills in an early childhood classroom.

SUMMARY OF QUALIFICATIONS

* Highly organized, motivated and patient.

* Able to train and guide young children in their academic pursuits.

* Thorough knowledge of computers - IBM PC, Lotus 1-2-3, and WordPerfect.

* Notably skilled in speaking and writing French.

* Excellent rapport with all levels of employees.

EDUCATION

Fitchburg State College, Fitchburg, Massachusetts.

SEMINARS

Massachusetts Early Childhood Foreign Language Education.

REFERENCES

Excellent professional and personal references upon request.

PROFESSIONAL RESUME

Richard J. Stewart
34 Ding Crossing
Indianapolis, IN 46227
(317) 555 - 7654

CAREER OBJECTIVE

Secure a position teaching High School Biology.

EDUCATION

Ball State University, Muncie, IN
B.S., May 1991, Major: Biology, Minor: Education

WORK EXPERIENCE

Summer 1988 & 1989

Indiana Bureau of Land Management
* Wetlands - Delineation, 1988 permitting
* Conducted Educational Tours of Wetlands

Summer 1990

Student Conservation Association Volunteer
* Stream and Timber Management
* Bat Study
    Seventy-five percent of activity was spent in remote areas with minimal supervision. Extensive use of topographical maps and aerial photographs were utilized.

Summer 1991

Assistant Biologist, Ball State University
* Fish Taxonomy, Electrofishing, Seining
* Statistics: I.J.W.B., I.B.I., SAS Computer Systems

RELATED EXPERIENCE

1985 to present

During this period, I have spent much of my spare time in the outdoors. Some of my activities include: bird watching, plant identification, hunting, fishing, studying animal behavior, insect collecting and keeping a field journal.

STANFORD UNIVERSITY
CAREER PLANNING AND PLACEMENT CENTER
STANFORD, CALIFORNIA 94305

DATE: October 1991

NAME:
PRESENT
ADDRESS:

Ann M. Gisler
312 High Drive
Stanford, CA 94305

TELEPHONE: (415) 555-7802

PERMANENT
ADDRESS:

4780 Green Street
Stanford, CA 94303

TELEPHONE: (415) 555-6234

OBJECTIVE: A position teaching reading in a reading lab of a school corporation.

EDUCATION:

9/89-6/91   Stanford University, Stanford, CA
             Reading Specialist Degree

3/85-2/89   Purdue University, Lafayette, IN
             B.S., Elementary Education

EXPERIENCE:

6/90-to the   Stanford University, Early Childhood Laboratory School
Present   Teaching Assistant

6/87-9/88   Purdue University, Department of Childhood Education, Lafayette,
              Indiana, day care provider

ADDITIONAL INFORMATION:

            Advisor: David Allen Fisher
            Interests: Skiing, hiking

```
                                    Vita
                              Ryan Farrell
```

Office Address   Home Address
Computer Science Dept.   876 Crestwood Dr.
University of Virginia   Charlottesville,
Virginia 22903 Charlottesville,   Virginia 22903
(804) 555 - 8976   (804) 555 - 7684

Principal Areas of Interest: Programming Languages, Software
                                          Engineering, Operating Systems,
                                          Programming Environments, and Real-Time
                                          Process Control.

Education:

1986-present: PH.D. candidate in Computer Science, University of
                     Virginia

   Currently employed as research assistant by Professor L. Gisler Thesis
   topic: Five-dimensional representations of four-dimensional programming
   languages. Principle areas of research: Software engineering and applied
   semantics.

Presentations:

* A departmental seminar at the University of Virginia, Fall, 1990
* Special ACM workshop on parallelism in four-dimensional languages, Spring
  1990
* University of Virginia, June, 1989
* Far West Symposium on Programming Languages and Systems, Fall, 1988.

Teaching (C.S. - related):

* Supervised programming languages seminar, spring, 1987.
* Developed and taught 1st-year student orientation course (autumn, 1986).
  Class covered Unix and HP program development utilities and programming
  methodology.

Lecturing (C.S. - related):

* Various lectures on denotational semantics three straight years -
  (Foundations of Languages)
* Three lectures on five-dimensional program graphs (Compilers and
  Optimization) Consulting:

   Consulted with individuals at College of William and Mary, Fall, 1990,
   about algorithm for parallelizing four-dimensional languages.

Computer-Related Work Experience:

1977-1984:   Programmer/analyst, systems analyst, Stemco Inc.,
                    Longview, TX

Worked with the bar division's process control group. Primary
responsibility was the Bruin 1/15, a PDP-11/10-based computer that
controlled the widget furnaces:

* Troubleshot the Bruin 1/15 operating system;
* Developed loadable communications link from the 1/15 to a PDP 11/45;
* Troubleshot users' programs;
* Rewrote University of Virginia's plot software;
* Developed a software development environment for the 1/15 that ran
  under DEC's RSX 11/M operating system. Environment included simulation
  of parts of the 1/15 operating system and downline-loading software for
  Bruin 1/15 source code.

Other programming work at University of Virginia:

* Developed a single-user operating system for an 8090-based computer;
* Developed an overlayed FORTRAN operator interface program for RSX-11/M;
* Acquired, installed, and maintained programming tools from the DEC
  user's group (DECUS).

1976-1977:   Programmer, University of Virginia

Wrote report-generating programs for the Alumni Office. The Alumni
Office's database, a hierarchical, Unix-based database, was developed at
the University of Virginia.

Research Reference

Professor Les Gisler
Computer Science Dept.
University of Virginia
Charlottesville, Virginia 22903
(804) 555 - 7787

KARLI ROSE
8340 Los Robles Road
Fishers, Indiana 46038
(317) 555-8044

CAREER OBJECTIVE:

An assistant principal position in an elementary school that will effectively utilize my creativity, organization, and enthusiasm.

EDUCATION:

INITIAL PRINCIPAL'S LICENSE, POST-GRADUATE STUDIES IN SCHOOL ADMINISTRATION, Butler University, Indianapolis, Indiana. Graduated December 1991 from the Experiential Program for Preparing School Principals (E.P.P.S.P.)

MASTER OF SCIENCE IN ELEMENTARY EDUCATION, Butler University, Indianapolis, Indiana. August 1986.

BACHELOR OF SCIENCE IN ELEMENTARY EDUCATION, Butler University, Indianapolis, Indiana. May 1980.

EXPERIENCE:

1988-Present   THIRD GRADE TEACHER, North Elementary, Noblesville Schools, Noblesville, Indiana. Utilized a variety of teaching strategies (cooperative learning, whole group instruction, 4MAT learning styles) to teach the core curriculum to multi-ability students in a self-contained classroom.

1985-1988   FIFTH GRADE TEACHER, North Elementary, Noblesville Schools, Noblesville, Indiana. Incorporated team teaching and computer literacy in teaching the core curriculum. Students were ability grouped as a grade level for math and reading.

Karli Rose
Page 1

Karli Rose
Page 2

1983-85   FOURTH GRADE TEACHER, Clewiston Primary and
           Intermediate Schools, Hendry County Schools,
           Clewiston, Florida. Created a peer tutoring system
           and individualized the curriculum to meet the
           needs of multi-cultural, low achieving students.

1983-81   ADMINISTRATIVE SECRETARY AND VOLUNTEER TUTOR,
           New Hope of Indiana, Indianapolis, Indiana.
           Tutored Pike High School students in math and
           reading in this residential facility that serves the
           mentally/physically handicapped.

1981   SECOND GRADE TEACHER, Crooked Creek School,
           Metropolitan School District of Washington
           Township, Indianapolis, Indiana. Filled a three
           month leave of absence and performed all duties
           of a regular classroom teacher.

1980-81   SUBSTITUTE TEACHER, Metropolitan School District of
           Washington Township. Contributed to the learning
           process in all elementary grade levels by
           administering the regular teacher's plans, grading
           papers, and giving feedback for follow-up.

PRESENTATIONS:

LEARNING AND LIVING IN FUTURE EDUCATION (L.I.F.E.)
CONFERENCE, Butler University, Indianapolis,
Indiana, 1991. The presentation was entitled
"Lifesaver--The Leader as a Visionary."
Information was shared on attributes of an
effective leader.

WHOLE GROUP INSTRUCTION IN READING, Noblesville
Schools, 1991. Information was shared on ways to
implement whole group instruction, grading, and
benefits to students.

Maria P. Day
1876 West Kessler
Carmel, IN   46032
(317) 555-1583

POSITION   DESIRED: Kindergarten Teacher

OBJECTIVES:

To obtain a position teaching
kindergarten or elementary
education.
To obtain a coaching position in girls
elementary school athletics.

EDUCATION:

Northwestern University
Bachelor of Science Degree (1974)
Major: Elementary Education
Endorsement: Kindergarten
GPA: 3.8, Major: 3.98

CERTIFICATION: Substitute Teacher's License 12/90

WORK   EXPERIENCE:

Little Lamb Day School, Carmel, IN
Teacher 's Assistant
6/90 - 8/91

**OFFICE   HELD/
MEMBERSHIP:**   Chairman for Alpha Chi Omega
Sorority

MARGARET M. STILES

1426 Green Street
Indianapolis, Indiana 46220
(317) 555-4988

PROFESSIONAL GOALS:

Teaching and coaching positions in Junior High or Secondary
School. Working toward an Athletic Administrative position
at the Secondary level.

TEACHING EXPERIENCE:

Northeastern Wayne School, Dayton, OH
- Physical Education, Junior High and High
  School
  10 years' experience

- Health Education, Junior High and High School
  16 years' experience

- Driver's Education
  10 years' experience

- Physical Education Department Chairman

- North Central Conference Evaluation Chairman
  for Health Education Department

- Curriculum Development - Health Education
  and Driver's Education

COACHING EXPERIENCE:

Northeastern Wayne High School, Dayton, OH
- Boy's Junior Varsity Basketball
  5 years
- Girl's Junior Varsity Basketball
  3 years
- Junior High Basketball
  4 years
- Varsity Tennis
  8 years

EDUCATION:

Bachelor of Science Degree, 1975, Purdue University
- Major: Physical Education
- Minor: Health Education

PROFESSIONAL ORGANIZATIONS:

- National Association of Secondary School Coaches
- Association for Supervision and Curriculum Development
- Indiana Secondary School Coaches
- American Red Cross Water Safety Instructor
- American Heart Association - Basic Life Support
- Sponsor: Students Against Drinking and Driving

LICENSES AND CERTIFICATION:

Indiana Teaching Licenses
- Elementary Education, 1-6, non-departmentalized 7/8
- Health & Safety Education, 5-12
- Physical Education, K-12

Ohio Teaching Licenses
- Physical Education, K-12
- Health & Safety Education, K-12
- American Red Cross Certification
- Standard First Aid; C.P.R.; Water Safety Instructor; Instructor of Lifeguard Training; and Babysitting Instructor.

REFERENCES:

Available upon request

JOANNA MORRIS
8860 RIVERSIDE ROAD
KALAMAZOO, MICHIGAN 40084
(616) 555-7224

PROFESSIONAL OBJECTIVE: TEACHING PRIMARY EDUCATION

EDUCATION: BACHELOR OF SCIENCE, WESTERN MICHIGAN UNIVERSITY
KALAMAZOO, MICHIGAN, DECEMBER 1989

ASSOCIATE OF ARTS, KALAMAZOO VALLEY COMMUNITY
COLLEGE KALAMAZOO, MICHIGAN, MAY 1985

MAJOR: ELEMENTARY EDUCATION
MINORS: MATH/SCIENCE, ENGLISH

CONSIDERABLE WORK IN TUTORING IN MATH, SCIENCE,
READING AND LANGUAGE ARTS

EXPERIENCE:

1985 -
present
NC LEARNING CENTER, KALAMAZOO, MICHIGAN
TUTORING STUDENTS IN PRE-KINDERGARTEN THROUGH
EIGHTH GRADE IN SUBJECTS SUCH AS MATH, SCIENCE,
READING, AND LANGUAGE ARTS.

1971 - 1983 DEPT. OF SOCIAL SERVICES, KALAMAZOO, MICHIGAN
FOSTER PARENT, KEEPING CHILDREN IN MY HOME.

1971 - 1983 EATON CORPORATION, KALAMAZOO, MICHIGAN
BEGAN AS A CLERK-TYPIST IN THE TOOL DESIGN
DEPARTMENT AND PROGRESSED THROUGH THE
CLERICAL RANKS IN TOOL DESIGN. METHODS AND
PROCESS ENGINEERING, ACCOUNTING, AND PAYROLL
DEPARTMENT.

1970 - 1971 ALLIED ALUMINUM COMPANY, SOUTH BEND, INDIANA
CLERK-TYPIST KEEPING RECORDS ON PART NUMBERS
(FENDERS, BUMPERS, AND BRAKES) AND TYPING
INVOICES.

1969 - 1970 0AKLAND COMMUNITY COLLEGE, BLOOMFIELD, MICHIGAN
WORKED AS A CLERK-TYPIST, PERFORMING
VARIOUS CLERICAL DUTIES SUCH AS TYPING, AND
OPERATING VARIOUS OFFICE MACHINES.

INTEREST: EXERCISING, READING, SEWING, SWIMMING AND
TUTORING CHILDREN AND ADULTS IN VARIOUS
SUBJECTS.

REFERENCES:

(BY PERMISSION)

MRS. REBA WIGGINS, TEACHER
863 FIRST STREET
BENTON HARBOR, MI 44022

MR. DAVID SPILLER, ATTORNEY AT LAW
55 SOUTH ROAD
KALAMAZOO, MI 40084

MISS MARGARET GISLER, REGISTERED NURSE
199 8TH STREET
KALAMAZOO, MI 40084

Dori Kriler Davis
1155 Ivy Lane
Indianapolis, Indiana 46220
(317) 555-3344

Education:

COLLEGE OF MOUNT ST. JOSEPH
    Bachelor of Arts May, 1978, 3.42 G.P.A.
    Major: Physical Education, Minor: Biology

MIAMI UNIVERSITY
    Master of Arts, August, 1979
    Majors: Physical Education and Recreation Administration

I.U.P.U.I./BUTLER UNIVERSITY
    Teacher Certification, May 1991, 3.95 G.P.A.
    Area: Elementary Education

Relevant Experience:

BUTLER UNIVERSITY
    Graduate Assistant College of Education, 1990 - present
    Team taught undergraduate preservice reading and language arts
    methods block and supervised afterschool tutoring practicum. Helped
    develop innovative undergraduate elementary/early childhood
    preservice program.

    Program Coordinator Project Leadership-Service, July, 1988 - August,
    1990
    Provided training and supervision of two hundred students and
    teachers for youth empowerment through mentoring, community
    service, and leadership development.

BOYS AND GIRLS CLUB
    Unit Director/Program Director, September, 1983 - July, 1988
    Designed and coordinated all aspects of afterschool and summer
    programs for youth, ages six through eighteen. Involved in
    curriculum development and implementation, membership
    recruitment, retention, and recognition, program publicity, community
    relations, and staff development.

NOBLESVILLE JUNIOR HIGH SCHOOL
Physical Education Teacher, February 1984 - May, 1984
Four-month contract to fill a maternity leave vacancy.

PRESTERA CENTER FOR MENTAL HEALTH SERVICES
Community Support Program Developer, October 1982 - September, 1983
Carried out a one-year grant for expansion of Community Support System for the chronically mentally ill in four-county catchment area. Served as coordinator of employment and social adjustment education program.

References upon request

Peggy Gisler
1419 Douglas Drive
Indianapolis, IN 46032
(317) 555 - 8976

Professional Goals:

- To run a University Reading Center.
- To help students studying in the field of education to know the real importance of reading.
- To help students to learn the latest methods of teaching reading.
- To help students to become comfortable with their own ability to teach reading to children of all ages.

Teaching Experiences:

Ball State University, Graduate Class, Reading 408
- Introductory class for students who are working on Reading Endorsement, Masters in Reading, or Reading Specialists Degree.

Springhill Elementary School, Greencastle, IN
- Reading Teacher.

Butler University Graduate Assistant
- Ran the Butler Reading Center for the summer.

Indianapolis Public School 105, Greencastle, IN
- First grade teacher for ten years.

Country Day School, Indianapolis, IN
- Kindergarten teacher for five years.

Licenses and Certification:

- Indiana Teaching License
- Elementary Education Grades 1-6
- Reading Specialist Degree
- American Red Cross Certification
- Standard First Aid and C.P.R.

Professional Committees

- Reading and Handwriting Adoption Committee
  Developed Criteria for adoption of new series, chose
  books, and revised curriculum guide.

- Indiana Reading Association

- Orton Society

References

Available upon Request

JAMIE C. DAY   (404) 555-9648
6285 BARFIELD RD.
ATLANTA, GA 30328

OBJECTIVE---
     Seeking a teaching position in High School Mathematics.

PERSONAL ATTRIBUTES--

     * HARDWORKING, WITH AN EXCELLENT ACADEMIC BACKGROUND AND A
       DEPENDABLE EMPLOYMENT HISTORY.

     * TAKES PRIDE IN WORK, AND EAGER TO TAKE ON NEW
       RESPONSIBILITIES WITH THE INTENTION OF SEEING EVERY PROJECT
       TO A SUCCESSFUL END.

ACADEMIC QUALIFICATIONS--

                BACHELOR OF SCIENCE IN MATHEMATICS
                       MINOR IN EDUCATION
                ROSE HULLMAN INSTITUTE OF TECHNOLOGY
                           MAY 1989

PERTINENT COURSE WORK--

Statistical Methods   Numerical Analysis
Operations Research   Probability
Linear Algebra   Calculus
Discrete & Combinatorial Algebra   Differential Equations
Fortran

                ROSE HULLMAN SCHOLARSHIP RECIPIENT

EMPLOYMENT HISTORY---

1989-91   SUMMERS STATE FARM, INDIANAPOLIS, IN

          FARM WORKER who gained experience and proficiency.
          Was put in charge of checking the work of twenty to
          twenty-five employees, as well as reporting to the
          employer.

1988-89   ARCHERS MEAT PACKING, FISHER, IN

          CLEANUP PERSON/MEAT PACKER responsible for assuring
          the sanitary conditions of the plant for each day's
          use.

1986-88   TYNERS FARM, CARMEL, IN

          FARM WORKER responsible for daily activities
          involving the various aspects of farm production
          and maintenance.

1985-86   MARION COUNTY FAIR, INDIANAPOLIS, IN

          MAINTENANCE WORKER whose duties include preparing
          display buildings, completing construction repairs,
          and maintenance.

ADDITIONAL INFORMATION---

          *   ENJOY SWIMMING, SOFTBALL, FOOTBALL

JOHN J. ALLEN

Present Address
765 5th Street
Washington, D.C. 20016-8001
(202) 555 - 2213

Permanent Address
28 Octavia Trail
Carmel, IN 46032
(317) 555 - 6675

OBJECTIVE   Full-time teaching position in telecommunications research and development, particularly in optical fiber networks, satellite communications or antenna design.

EDUCATION   **University of Washington**
Currently pursuing Masters of Science in Electrical Engineering with a concentration in telecommunications and fiber optics.
Expected Graduation: June, 1992

Whitman College
Bachelors of Science with Highest Distinction in Electrical Engineering, May, 1989

EXPERIENCE
1989-1990   **University of Washington Dept. of Electrical Engineering**
TEACHING ASSISTANT: Controls Courses and Intro to Electronics Lab.

Summer 1990   **Amoco Incorporated,** Washington, D.C.,
SPECIAL TECHNICAL ASSISTANT: Installed hardware and software for computer control of test equipment; conducted stress tests on circuit boards; wrote software to capture and plot oscilloscope waveforms.

Summer 1989   **Naylor Pipe Company,** Chicago, IL.
SENIOR STAFF TECHNOLOGIST: Conducted research on optical fiber communication systems. Primary research was an experimental study of privacy and security issues in passive, fiber-to-the-home networks.

ADDITIONAL INFORMATION
CAD tool experience: SPICE, MAGIC, IRSIM, and SUPREM
Member Tau Beta Pi and Pi Tau Sigma

Robert C. Norton
596 Walean Drive
St. Paul, MN 55631
(612) 555-1213

OBJECTIVE: To obtain a teaching position in either elementary education or with children who have special needs in reading.

EDUCATION: University of Minnesota, Minneapolis, MN
Currently in Masters program in Reading
Syracuse University, NY 9/87 - 5/-90
Bachelor of Science
Major: Elementary Education
Minor: Reading

EXPERIENCE:

Brentwood Elementary School: Student Teacher, Minneapolis, MN, January - March 1989
Grade 5. Student teaching responsibilities included: all teaching duties, attending staff and parent-teacher organization meetings, participating in textbook adoption sessions for Social Studies, attending Teacher In-Service day to evaluate performance-based accreditation.

Versailies State Park: Waterfront Director/Lifeguard, Versailes, IN, Summers, 1988 - 90

WFYI-TV Channel 20: Public Relations Intern, Indianapolis, IN January - May 1990
Researched and wrote history of the station, and assisted in Public Relations.

Syracuse University: Literary Magazine Editor, Syracuse, NY Fall 1988 - May 1990
Conducted staff meetings, selected published material, and designed the final layout

OTHER INFORMATION:

Sigma Tau Delta, English Honorary

John Newcombe Wright English Award ,Pascal, Excel

Chapter Six

SAMPLE COVER LETTERS

March 25, 1991

Clay School System
635 Industrial Drive, Suite 248
Wilkes Barre, PA 18711

Dear Sir:

This letter is in response to Sunday's advertisement in the
Gazette. I am interested in applying for full-time
employment as a school psychologist in the Wilkes-Barre area.
As you can see from my resume, I have a strong concentration
in the field of early childhood psychology.

I would like the opportunity to meet with you to discuss my
resume. I believe that I would be a productive addition to
your school system.

Sincerely,

John P. Whitehead

2234 Eden Hollow Road, Suite 5
Hayward, CA 94545
Office: (555) 552-7788
Fax: (555) 552-0098

April 27, 1991

John Boyd
Kinder-Care Learning Centers
7722 Oakwood Drive
Indianapolis, IN 46250

Dear John:

Your school interests me. I've researched it and found it to be
a very progressive school.

My family looks forward, as I, to making a change to
Indianapolis. If my strengths can help you, it would be my
pleasure to meet.

Please keep all contact personal and confidential.

Sincerely,

Michael K. Eberts

October 18, 1991

Human Resources Department
Council Bluffs Unified School District
8825 North Woodland Drive
Council Bluffs, Iowa 51503

To whom it may concern:

I am writing to inquire about any openings you may have for a director of your gifted and talented program. My experience in education includes a part-time kindergarten position and an endorsement in gifted education.

I am currently enrolled in the Principal Program at Iowa College. I have been a first grade teacher for the past twelve years; however, I am seeking a career change.

If you should have an interest in talking with me further, please contact me. My resume is enclosed for your review. Thank you.

Sincerely,

David Allen Perkins
5578 High Drive
Council Bluffs, Iowa 51504

2556 Broadlawn St.
Houston, TX 88674
May 27, 1991

Personnel Director
George Christopher School
Box 788964
San Francisco, CA 94178-8964

Dear Personnel Director,

Please consider my application for the position of School Psychologist. I have graduated from Notre Dame with a Bachelor of Science degree in Elementary Education and a Masters in Psychology. I have majors in both Reading and School Psychology.

I feel that my experience in the field of School Psychology and as Student Assistant in the Science Department, along with my education, qualifies me for a position with your school corporation. I will continue to be successful as a School Psychologist because I enjoy challenges, work hard, and am concerned with doing the best I can at all times.

I would like to have an interview to discuss how my placement with your school corporation will benefit both of us. Please phone me anytime at (218) 555-8866. I look forward to hearing from you.

Yours truly,

Edda Fisher

Enclosure

March 17, 1991

Franklin Central School Corporation.
255 Long Hill Rd.
Middletown, CT 06457

Dear Joe Osee:

I wish to apply for a position in your school corporation. I
graduated with a degree in Music Education. I have an extensive
and varied background working with the music in the
elementary school, which, combined with my schooling and personal
interest, could be very valuable to your school corporation.

I look forward to hearing from you. Enclosed is my resume.
Please feel free to call me and set up an interview at your
convenience.

Sincerely,

Jerry Glick
5544 Wildwood Drive
West Lake, Ohio 44145

1610 Willow Lane
New Haven, OH 57220
August 20, 1991

Mr. Detrick Cross
Supervisor, Special Education
Stafford Community School Corporation
132 West Street
Frankton, OH 57333

Dear Mr. Cross:

I understand you have an opening for a school psychologist.
Enclosed is my resume for your review.

If you find that I qualify for the position, I would greatly
appreciate the opportunity to talk with you.

Thank you for your consideration.

Sincerely,

Pamela S. Woods

enclosure

7810 Farrington, Ct. #689
Woodbridge, VA 22192
January 26, 1990

Mr. John Morris, Director of Personnel
Apple Valley Schools
743 Crescent Blvd.
Apple Valley, MN 56438

Dear Mr. Morris:

I am currently teaching in a self-contained third grade classroom in
Woodbridge, Virginia. I am enjoying my first year of teaching, but I am
interested in relocating back to the Midwest. In January 1988, I worked
as an intern at Cascade Elementary with JoAnne Walker. She suggested I
contact you concerning a teaching position with Apple Valley Schools. My
enthusiasm for teaching and my experiences, both collegiate and
professional, make me confident I can be a valuable addition to the Apple
Valley faculty.

Most recently, I have been developing my computer skills by
participating in inservices in LOGO instruction. I am currently attending
seminars at the University of Virginia on "LOGO in the Classroom".

By carefully selecting trade books, I have implemented whole-language
instruction in social studies and science. To further integrate language
arts into the entire curriculum, I have used learning logs and response
journals to incorporate reading/writing process teaching.

I am available anytime this Spring to meet with you and discuss
working for Apple Valley Schools. I currently have plans to be in
Minnesota in mid-February. I will call you on January 31st to schedule an
appointment. I appreciate your consideration.

Sincerely,

Bryce T. Stewart

enclosure

May 20, 1992
1516 North Central Avenue
Indianapolis, IN 46208
317-555-1962

Mr. James Day
Meridian School Corporation
9888 West Washington Blvd.
Monterey Park, CA 91754

Sir:

This letter is in reply to the advertisement in the <u>Monterey Star</u> on Sunday, May 24.

I earned a B.S. Degree in Elementary Education from Purdue University in May of this year. I have specialized in the fields of reading and learning disabilities. You will note, I have attached a qualifications summary and other pertinent data for your consideration.

I think that my experiences can be utilized by your school corporation to an advantage, and I look forward to an interview with you.

Sincerely,

Kathy Johnson

6225 High Drive
New Brunswick, NJ 08901

May 8, 1991

Dear Sir/Madam:

I am writing to you with the hope that you might have an
opening soon in your school corporation. If you don't, I
would very much appreciate your keeping my resume (enclosed)
on file for future opportunities.

I finished all my course work for a master's degree at
Harvard University and am presently writing a report on my
research project, "The Effects of Television on Children's
Reading."

I am a sincere, hard-working individual with a capacity to
learn quickly. I enjoy challenging work and am capable of
working under pressure. I believe I am the type of
professional you are seeking.

Thank you very much for taking the time to consider my
qualifications and candidature. I look forward to hearing
from you soon.

Sincerely Yours,

Charles D. Stiles

May 20, 1992

Louise M. Paugh
1624 Sawbridge Drive
Linden, N.J. 07036
201-555-1496

Mr. Andrew Scaruffi
Human Resources
Stoney Creek School Corporation
4499 Hyde Street
San Francisco, CA 94109

Dear Mr. Scaruffi:

I am writing in response to our telephone conversation about your opening for a high school English teacher. I am presently working at Washington High School in Linden, New Jersey. However, I am planning to relocate to San Francisco. After our informative telephone conversation, I believe that I have the qualifications your school corporation is seeking.

I presently have a month-to-month lease on my home in Linden. If I am selected to fill your corporation's vacancy for an English teacher, I am available for immediate employment. I would like to move to San Francisco at the earliest possible time.

I am looking forward to hearing from you. Enclosed is my resume.

Sincerely,

Louise M. Paugh

JILL R. MCCOY
473 HILL DRIVE WEST
KENOSHA, WI 53143
(414) 555-6320

April 24, 1991

Mr. Richard Serafini, Principal
Crestwood Elementary School
6341 Crestwood Drive
Naperville, IL 60565

Dear Mr. Serafini:

I will be graduating from the University of Wisconsin in May.
I am seeking an elementary school teaching position in
kindergarten.

My education from the University of Wisconsin has exposed me
to the latest developments in the teaching profession. It
has also given me the opportunity to participate in different
classroom situations. I plan to continue my professional
growth in the future by pursuing a master's degree in
education.

Enclosed, you will find my resume. A complete credentials
file is available upon request through University of
Wisconsin: Educational Placement Office, 4600 Sunset Avenue,
Madison, Wisconsin 53709, 608-555-3000.

I would like to request an interview with the Crestwood
School Corporation at this time. I may be contacted at my
home address. Could you please send me informational
literature on your school corporation? Thank you.

Sincerely,

Jill R. McCoy

Enclosure

Margaret Stiles

3033 Maple Drive
Minneapolis, MN 55410
Tel. (612) 555-1881

May 8, 1992

Ontario Valley School
5892 Burlington
Pasaic, New Jersey 07055

Dear Sir/Madam:

I am presently a graduate student at the Krannert
Graduate School of Education, Purdue University, working
towards a Master of Science degree in Elementary
Education. My date of graduation is July 7, 1992.

As my prior educational background and work experience
are in elementary education, the profile of your school
was provided to me by the staff of the Krannert Graduate
School Placement Office.

Needless to state, I am extremely interested in pursuing
the possibility of obtaining a position in a school such
as yours. I am particularly interested in working in the
lower elementary level.

I am enclosing my resume for your review. If you need
any additional information, please let me know and I
will be pleased to comply.

Looking forward to hearing from you.

Sincerely,

Margaret Stiles

Enclosure

Anthony H. Cohen
167 Tuxedo Drive
Redding, CT 06896
(203) 555-1678

February 8, 1991

Mr. George Smart
Director of Personnel
Vocational Technical College
8775 West Douglas Street
Virginia Beach, VA 23456

Dear Mr. Smart:

As I leave behind a most rewarding 10-year career with Washington School Corporation, I am ready to take on a new challenge in which my Education Specialist Degree in Reading can be beneficial.

During my career in the Washington Corporation, I have held the positions of reading teacher, Director of Reading, and Director of Communications. Being part of the communications industry has taught me the importance of providing a fast, accurate, and reliable service to the parents and teachers in a school corporation.

I would like the opportunity to talk with you about my background and the areas in which I can benefit your school corporation.

Sincerely,

Anthony H. Cohen

AHC/tbd

Enclosure

Elizabeth A. Grossa
1346 E. 22nd St. #105
Carbondale, IL 62901

February 28, 1991

Happy Hollow School Corporation
8465 Baker Street
Carbondale, IL 62901

To Whom It May Concern:

This letter is in response to the ad placed in the Carbondale
Gazette on May 26, 1991.

I will earn my B.S. degree in Elementary Education from
Southern Illinois University in August of 1991. I have
specialized in the field of Early Childhood Education and
also have a reading endorsement. Your ad was of particular
interest to me as the opening is for teachers in the
kindergarten area.

Enclosed is my resume detailing my work experience and
educational background. I feel that my qualifications would
be an asset to your corporation.

I would welcome the opportunity to meet with you to discuss
my experience and qualifications.

Sincerely,

Elizabeth A. Grossa

```
                        Anna P. Day
                     3345 Tenth Street
                  West Lafayette, IN 47906
```

June 9, 1991

```
Personnel Director
Pershing Township School Corporation
Lindenwood Ave.
Austin, TX 78501
```

Dear Personnel Director:

I read about your corporation in <u>The Texan State Journal</u>, and would like to inquire about employment opportunities as a nurse within your school district.

I will be graduating from Northwestern University in May of this year with a Bachelor of Science degree in Nursing. Throughout my collegiate career, I have maintained a balanced background of activities and academics. In addition, my past summer internship provided me with invaluable work experience in monitoring techniques and worker relations.

A copy of my resume is enclosed for your review. If you need further information, I will be more than happy to provide you with the necessary materials.

I know how busy you must be during this time of year, but I would appreciate a few minutes of your time. I may be reached at the above address or by calling (317) 555-2203. I look forward to hearing from you about my future with your school corporation.

Sincerely,

Anna P. Day

Enclosure: Resume

Martha Lombardi
45 Kelton Avenue, Apartment 5D
New York, New York 10024

March 10, 1992

Mr. Vincent Cabrillo
Human Resources Department
New York City Schools
12504 Madison Avenue
New York, New York 100290

Dear Mr. Cabrillo:

I am presently a VISTA volunteer working in School 98 in New York City. Pride in what I have been able to accomplish at this school compels me to apply for a job as a teacher in the New York City School system in order to continue helping disadvantaged children.

The enclosed resume shows that I have the appropriate licenses and experience for a position as an elementary school teacher in the New York City School system.

I bring to teaching enthusiasm, dedication, a solid academic background, and a willingness to become involved in the community where my students live.

I appreciate your consideration of my qualifications.

Sincerely,

Martha Lombardi

Mary Kaye LeBeau
110 Chestnut Avenue
Muncie, IN 46096
(317) 555-8747

January 24, 1991

Mr. Robert Myers, Principal
Ball Elementary School
2426 Oakwood Court
Muncie, IN 46246

Dear Mr. Myers:

My name is Mary Kaye LeBeau, and I am seeking an elementary
teaching position in your school system. My resume is enclosed.
I feel I have the experience, enthusiasm, and sensitivity towards
students' needs and circumstances to be considered for a teaching
position in your school system.

I have used the Assertive Discipline Program for the past five
years to instill responsibility and create a good learning
environment for my students. I am a dedicated teacher who
does many extra programs in her classroom. Some recent
programs I have been involved with are:

* Father's Breakfasts
* Grandparent's Day Gala
* Mother's Day Programs - Talent Shows
* Graduation for the "Class of 2000"
* Hobby Shows
* Screening program for Kindergarten
* New Handbook for Kindergarten

I believe in a classroom where it happens! I have a goal to
improve each year and have the willingness to try new ideas. I
love being a teacher and devote a great deal of my personal
time to my job. I look forward to sharing more of my ideas
with you. Please give me the opportunity!

Respectfully,

Mary Kaye LeBeau

Enclosure

Brian Washington
2556 Broadlawn Street
San Francisco, CA 94143

May 27, 1991

Ms. Julia Hernandez
Personnel Director
Mount Carmel High School
P.O. Box 788964
San Francisco, CA 94147-1959

Dear Ms. Hernandez:

Please consider my application for a teaching position in the Biology
Department at Mount Carmel. I have graduated from Notre Dame with a
Bachelor of Science degree in Education and a Master's in Biology.

I feel that my experience in the field of Biology and as Student Assistant
to the Science Department at Notre Dame, along with my education, qualifies
me for a position at Mount Carmel. I will continue to be successful as
a teacher because I enjoy challenges, work hard, and am concerned with doing
the best I can at all times.

I would like to have an interview to discuss how by placement with your
school will benefit both of us. Please phone me anytime at (415) 555-8866.
I look forward to hearing from you.

Sincerely,

Brian Washington

Enclosure

William Chamberlain
1422 North Senate
Chicago, IL 60615-5221

January 18, 1993

Father Thomas Clegg
Principal
Christ the King School
P.O. Box 887
Portland, OR 96437

Dear Father:

Are you looking for someone with experience in the area of reading?

After seeing your ad in the Portland Times, I believe I have the qualifications you are seeking for the position advertised on December 27, 1992. I believe that I could be the person you are looking for.

My attached resume describes my successful background in running the Northwestern University Reading Center and the New World Learning Center as well as my education degrees. These qualifications give me all the skills your school needs.

Sincerely yours,

William Chamberlain

CLARENCE SCOTT TALLEY III
600 Porter St.
Las Vegas, NV   89890
702/555-3893

February 8, 1992

Sam Richards
2023 Lombard Street
Saint Joseph, MO 64501
(816) 555-8653

Mark Andrews
Brookside Park School
56 West Street
St. Joseph, MO 64518

Dear Mr. Andrews:

Thank you for giving me the opportunity to visit your school and to
speak with you about the teaching position. After talking with you,
I am very interested in this position and would appreciate the
opportunity to work at Brookside Park. With my experience and
background in elementary education, I believe that I will be an
asset to your school.

Thank you for your time and consideration. I am looking forward to
hearing from you soon.

Sincerely,

Sam Richards

VGM CAREER BOOKS

CAREER DIRECTORIES
Careers Encyclopedia
Dictionary of Occupational Titles
Occupational Outlook Handbook

CAREERS FOR
Animal Lovers
Bookworms
Computer Buffs
Crafty People
Culture Lovers
Environmental Types
Film Buffs
Foreign Language Aficionados
Good Samaritans
Gourmets
History Buffs
Kids at Heart
Nature Lovers
Number Crunchers
Sports Nuts
Travel Buffs

CAREERS IN
Accounting; Advertising; Business; Child
Care; Communications; Computers;
Education; Engineering; Finance;
Government; Health Care; High Tech;
Law; Marketing; Medicine; Science;
Social & Rehabilitation Services

CAREER PLANNING
Beginning Entrepreneur
Career Planning & Development for
   College Students & Recent Graduates
Careers Checklists
Cover Letters They Don't Forget
Executive Job Search Strategies
Guide to Basic Resume Writing
Joyce Lain Kennedy's Career Book
Slam Dunk Resumes
Successful Interviewing for College
   Seniors

HOW TO
Approach an Advertising Agency and
   Walk Away with the Job You Want
Bounce Back Quickly After
   Losing Your Job
Change Your Career
Choose the Right Career
Get & Keep Your First Job
Get into the Right Law School
Get People to Do Things
   Your Way
Have a Winning Job Interview
Jump Start a Stalled Career
Land a Better Job
Launch Your Career in TV News
Make the Right Career Moves
Market Your College Degree
Move from College into a
   Secure Job
Negotiate the Raise
   You Deserve
Prepare a *Curriculum Vitae*
Prepare for College
Run Your Own Home Business.
Succeed in College
Succeed in High School
Write Successful Cover Letters
Write a Winning Resume
Write Your College
   Application Essay

OPPORTUNITIES IN
Accounting
Acting
Advertising

Aerospace
Agriculture
Airline
Animal & Pet Care
Architecture
Automotive Service
Banking
Beauty Culture
Biological Sciences
Biotechnology
Book Publishing
Broadcasting
Building Construction Trades
Business Communication
Business Management
Cable Television
CAD/CAM
Carpentry
Chemistry
Child Care
Chiropractic
Civil Engineering
Cleaning Service
Commercial Art & Graphic Design
Computer Maintenance
Computer Science
Counseling & Development
Crafts
Culinary
Customer Service
Data Processing
Dental Care
Desktop Publishing
Direct Marketing
Drafting
Electrical Trades
Electronic & Electrical Engineering
Electronics
Energy
Engineering
Engineering Technology
Environmental
Eye Care
Fashion
Fast Food
Federal Government
Film
Financial
Fire Protection Services
Fitness
Food Services
Foreign Language
Forestry
Government Service
Health & Medical
High Tech
Home Economics
Homecare Services
Hospital Administration
Hotel & Motel Management
Human Resource Management
Information Systems
Installation & Repair
Insurance
Interior Design
International Business
Journalism
Laser Technology
Law
Law Enforcement & Criminal
   Justice
Library & Information Science
Machine Trades
Magazine Publishing
Marine & Maritime
Masonry
Marketing
Materials Science
Mechanical Engineering
Medical Imaging
Medical Technology

Metalworking
Military
Modeling
Music
Newspaper Publishing
Nonprofit Organizations
Nursing
Nutrition
Occupational Therapy
Office Occupations
Packaging Science
Paralegal
Paramedical
Part-time & Summer Jobs
Performing Arts
Petroleum
Pharmacy
Photography
Physical Therapy
Physician
Plastics
Plumbing & Pipe Fitting
Postal Service
Printing
Property Management
Psychology
Public Health
Public Relations
Purchasing
Real Estate
Recreation & Leisure
Refrigeration & Air Conditioning
Religious Service
Restaurant
Retailing
Robotics
Sales
Secretarial
Securities
Social Science
Social Work
Speech-Language Pathology
Sports & Athletics
Sports Medicine
State & Local Government
Teaching
Technical Writing &
   Communications
Telecommunications
Telemarketing
Television & Video
Theatrical Design & Production
Tool & Die
Transportation
Travel
Trucking
Veterinary Medicine
Visual Arts
Vocational & Technical
Warehousing
Waste Management
Welding
Word Processing
Writing
Your Own Service Business

RESUMES FOR
Advertising Careers
Banking and Financial Careers
College Students &
   Recent Graduates
Communications Careers
Education Careers
Engineering Careers
Environmental Careers
Health and Medical Careers
High School Graduates
High Tech Careers
Midcareer Job Changes
Sales and Marketing Careers
Scientific and Technical Careers

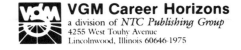
VGM Career Horizons
a division of *NTC Publishing Group*
4255 West Touhy Avenue
Lincolnwood, Illinois 60646-1975